THE RIVER RATS
OF VIETNAM

THE RIVER RATS OF VIETNAM

CHRISTINE & MARK PURDY

AuthorHouse™
1663 Liberty Drive
Bloomington, IN 47403
www.authorhouse.com
Phone: 1-800-839-8640

First published by AuthorHouse 8/12/2010

ISBN: 978-1-4520-5495-7 (sc)

Library of Congress Control Number: 2010912047

Printed in the United States of America

DEDICATION

My name is Mark Purdy, and there was a period in my life that I have avoided talking about for many years. But, I feel now, more then ever, that I should get past my own… well whatever you want to call it, that prevented me from discussing these events till now. Some people might call it fear, others might call it burying the past. Personally, I don't know what my reasons were. I just know that I find myself finally able to talk about this horrendous time in my life. And, with the help of my Wife, I would like to introduce you to a seldom-talked about group of men known as…

"THE RIVER RATS OF VIETNAM."

When you read most books on the Vietnam Conflict you read about the tunnel rats, or the marines on the battlefields, or the other various military outfits that were called to duty as I was. However, very little has been written about us River Rats and that needs to change because we played such an important role throughout the U.S. involvement over there. Now don't get me wrong, everyone that served over there deserves all the credit they are given and I do not wish to belittle or discredit any of those brave men and women. I just feel that we River Rats need to have our story told as well.

That having been said, I would like to honor all my fellow River Rats with a saying that holds a special meaning among all of my Vietnam brother/sisters in arms.

To all those who paid the ultimate sacrifice.
And, for all those who survived that horrendous ordeal....

WELCOME HOME!

CONTENTS

CHAPTER I

LIFE BEFORE BASICS

In my early high school years I can remember President Kennedy explaining through several news casts that we as a nation would not enter the conflict in Vietnam. That all changed with three shots on November 22, 1963.

Shortly after Lyndon Banes Johnson took the oath of the presidency, he announced his plans to reverse President Kennedy's U.S. commitment to abstain from getting involved in Vietnam. I knew he sealed my fate when he announced his intentions of sending as many troupes as needed to help train the S.V. (Southern Vietnamese) in defense tactics so as to protect themselves against the more powerful N. V. (North Vietnamese).

By 1966, the reports of actions in the split country of Vietnam were getting worse by the day. The subject was covered by all forms of the media, and one could not help but notice the contradictions from one broadcast to the next. For example, one news report would tell of how our service men and women were fighting communism in order to help the general public of Vietnam. While another would report of how we were not achieving any strategical objective, be it political or otherwise, and how we should bring our troops home before anymore lives were lost.

Personally, I didn't know what to think. I understood the general concept of stopping communism, and if our presence in Vietnam meant that we were doing our part to stop it from growing any stronger then it already was, then I was all for it. But on the other hand, I was scared to death to go thousands of miles from home to fight a battle that I knew I really didn't understand.

Looking back, I can even remember times when the subject was brought up in some of my classes. The teachers all seemed to put the "stopping communism" spin on the whole situation, but as a senior in high school facing the possibility of going to war for my country, I was not entirely convinced they were right. I agreed that everyone needed to do his or her part to stop the growing threat of communism, and, seeing how "we are the United States" we surely could beat a third world country like Vietnam. But was the cost of war really worth it? After all, if Vietnam was a third world country, how much impact could they have on a country as strong as the United States? I would soon realize how truly wrong my thinking was.

During that last year of high school, the subject of Vietnam was everywhere. You couldn't escape it. Even when I was with my buddies, as young as we were, we would talk about the appending draft. We all knew we would each be called on to serve our country soon after we graduated. Our banter would revolve around anything from whether we would join the reserves of a certain branch so we could try and go where we wanted, or just wait to be drafted and let the cards fall where they may. But through all our egotistical teenage crap, we all knew that it was an individual decision, and one that could not be made in haste.

Shortly after our high school graduation we all started getting our draft cards. Whenever one of us got one, we would talk about what draft numbers we had and what exactly that number meant. For me, getting that draft card made the whole Vietnam thing seem more real.

By then we all knew how the whole draft system worked. Once a week there would be a set of draft numbers selected. Since they were going in order, it was easy to tell when your number would be called, and as you can well imagine, the closer our numbers came, the more we realized we had to make some life and death decisions and we had to make them fast. After all, the way in which you served could make all the difference in the world.

What made these decisions even harder was the fact that we all knew someone who did not make it back. Or, when they did make it back, even when they came back in one piece, they suffered from the mental anguishes from what they experienced in a strange land filled with people they did not understand. But the biggest complaint a returning soldier most often had, even worse than their Vietnam experiences, were the verbal outcries from their fellow Americans once they came home.

Some soldiers could not understand why they were hated so much by people who could not possibly understand the ordeal that service men/women were subjected to in this foreign land. After all, many of them did not volunteer to go over there. They were forced by their government to fight a battle they did not want to fight. So why were they being held accountable for something they had no control over? Some veterans even went so far as to deny even going over there just so they didn't have to endure the humiliation that others had to deal with.

My buddies and I sure did a lot of soul searching while trying to figure out just what we were going to do. Some of us even contemplated trying to avoid the draft all together. We all heard of ways to avoid being called to duty, and some of us thought long and hard about using one of them. Things like having flat feet, or if you already had a sibling serving in Vietnam, or maybe even if you were a college student with passing grades, or married with children. Basically there were many alternatives to being forced into the draft.

As for myself? Well I was not so worried about whether I would be called to duty, getting my draft card took care of that. It was now more a matter of "how" I would serve my country that cluttered my typical teenage mind. I guess you could say that I felt if I was going to be forced into all this, then at least I was going to say how and where I was going to serve. I wanted to at least make that decision for myself.

While trying to decide on which branch of the service I wanted to join, I started thinking about my father. I would like to say that his participation during World War II was a direct influence on that decision, but that is not true. He never really talked about his role in those days. His stories were more based on his relationship with my mother and the risks and efforts they took to see each other, rather then focusing on the realities of war he undoubtedly faced everyday.

You see my father, Dee Purdy, served during World War II in the 8ᵗʰ Army/Air Force division, where he was responsible for loading the ammo onto the B17 bomber planes. He was stationed in England were he met and married my mother Pam Griffin on December 12, 1945; she was 18 and he was 27. But that is pretty much all I really knew about his life there. Whenever my two younger brothers, Bryn and Ross, or I would ask him about his war time experiences, he would give very direct and simple answers. I wouldn't say he refused to answer our questions; it was more like he wanted to protect his sons from the realities of what his life was truly like back then. I do, however, remember him telling me one story about how some of the pilots would hold onto life just long enough to bring down their planes safely then died before they could be removed from their cockpits. But more importantly, I remember him saying that he was glad not to be involved in the daily combat of the war, and how proud he was to have served his country.

I did ask him his opinion on what I should do and I remember him telling me it was my decision, but not to make that decision in haste. In the end, I decided that the Navy held the best options for me. I was even told that by joining the Naval reserves I would be able to have some say as to where I would be stationed, and, like my dad, I did not want to be involved with the daily combat of war life, so the Navy it was.

After talking to a recruiter I found out that the large battleships were not being used for much combat during the Vietnam conflict. Well, at that time anyway, and that was just fine by me. I even half heartedly thought I might get to do some traveling and see parts of the world I might not otherwise get a chance to see.

It was well known that the large ships traveled all over the world, and that the men and women aboard were often allowed to leave the ships at various ports of call. Traveling, seeing the world, and just being on the ocean sounded exciting to me. So, at the tender age of 21, I decided to join the Milwaukee Wisconsin Naval reserves. Now the hard part; telling my family.

My Mom and Dad, who remembered all too well the tribulations of WWII, were adamantly against our nation's involvement in the Vietnam conflict. This made telling them about my wanting to enlist even harder, but I knew deep down that they would appreciate my coming to them first and letting them voice their opinions. They were not exactly thrilled with the idea of their oldest son going off to war, but they did understand my reasoning for joining the reserves.

My Mom and Dad raised my brothers and me to believe this country was a great place to be, because we had freedoms that many other countries did not have. They made sure that we attended church services every Sunday morning and instilled in us a strong faith in the Lord. Part of that faith was to help those that needed it. I told myself that the people of Vietnam needed to be saved. They needed to enjoy the freedoms we enjoyed here in the United States. It wasn't until I actually got over there that I realized how foolish those ideas really were.

So off to the local recruiting station I went and joined the naval reserves. After the recruiter gave his spiel about Navy life, he gave me a packet of papers and explained that I was going to serve for four years and that I should take the packet home, look it over, and come back when I had it all filled out.

When I returned with all my T's crossed and I's dotted, the recruiter told me to report to my training classes which were held every Monday night. That first night we were all sworn in and I knew my life as a Navy man had truly begun.

It was about this time that I met my first wife Phyllis. We were both attending the New Tribes Bible Institute and we started spending as much time together as we could. She was a cute little redhead and I found myself drawn to her. Soon after, we both decided to advocate from the institute, and were married in a simple church ceremony attended by only family and a few close friends.

We moved into a lower Polish flat in South Milwaukee that was owned at that time by my parents. Phyllis and I both worked for my Uncle Kay at Purdy Steaks making very little money, and I was still attending my reservist meetings every Monday night. All in all I guess you could say we were living a very simple quiet life, and were genuinely happy. Until one day...

CHAPTER 2

LEAVING FOR BASICS

During one of my regular reservist meetings the leader of our group passed out slips of paper with various naval ships typed on them, [submarine, carrier, destroyer, aircraft carrier]. They told us to mark in numerical order which ships we would be most interested in serving on in the event our status would change from inactive to active. I chose the naval vessels that I thought would guarantee me the most amount of foreign travel. After we turned in these papers the leader told us to pack your gear your heading for Treasure Island in Vallejo, California to await your orders.

After that meeting was over I headed home to tell my new bride of my active status. I knew this was coming, but that didn't change the uneasy feeling I had in the pit of my stomach. I started thinking about how we were barely making ends meet. How was she going to make it with me gone? Would I be able to get money to her if she needed it and would it be enough to pay the bills? After all, the military didn't pay much and it was not like I could come home on the weekends to a part time job.

When I finally made it home that night Phyllis was watching TV as usual. I sat down held her hand and we talked all night long. We decided that there was nothing we could do about it now so we did the only thing we could do; we started getting ready for me to leave.

The next thing I knew I had to do was tell my mom and dad. For some reason, that was even harder then telling Phyllis. My Mom took the news as well as any mother would, I guess. She didn't want to make it any harder on me then it already was, but I could tell how scared she was. Not so much by what she said, but by what she did not say. Dad just listened and told me to remember that God had my back and to remember to take my Bible. They both told me they would be praying for me and somehow that gave me a sense of comfort.

The powers that be gave me a couple of weeks to get my affairs in order and Phyllis and I spent as much of that time together as we could. We tried to cram a lifetime of memories into two weeks. We went out dancing and spent hours just holding each other for all we were worth, then it came: My last night home. I wanted to spend that last night alone with my wife, and thankfully my family understood. Phyllis helped me pack my gear and tried to hide her tears.

The day I left I told her I did not want her to go to the airport with me. I didn't want the public emotional scene that always comes with a husbands' final farewell to his wife. In the end, I decided it would be best if my father would take me.

The next morning my father came to pick me up and, after a final goodbye to my bride, I got into my father's car and we traveled the 15 minutes to the airport in an understood silence. Neither one of us wanted to say what we both knew needed to be said. Instead we just sat letting the silence do the talking for us. When we finally got to the airport I turned back to my Dad and said "thanks for the ride Dad," grabbed my gear and headed for the terminal. If my Dad said anything I didn't hear him.

When I got to the airport I had two surprises waiting for me. The first surprise was to see that four of my friends from the reservist meeting were on the same flight. The second was that we were flying commercially. We passed the time talking about what we each thought boot camp was going to be like and where we each thought we would end up. We all wanted to be assigned to the big carriers and we laughed and joked about what countries we would see and what we would do when we reached each port of call.

When we landed at the San Francisco airport we were surprised to see various military men holding up signs that said Treasure Island. We would find out later that some of the men stationed at Treasure Island would make a few bucks on the side by transporting incoming men to base in their own vehicles. My buddies and I decided to pay the $.25 to take the shuttle instead, which is what our orders told us to do anyway.

When we got to the base we were escorted by the M.P.'s to our check in point. We were given our bunk numbers and told to remember that number because that number became who we were. The M.P.'s then showed us where we were to stand for our daily morning check in. It was just a bunch of numbers painted on the ground right outside the barracks.

After we were given our bedding, which consisted of a pillowcase, 2 sheets, and 2 scratchy wool blankets, we were told to make our bunks and hit the sack.

The next morning at 0500 revelry was blasted over the intercom yelling for us to get our asses out of bed. We knew we only had 10 minutes to get to our check in point so we jumped up got dressed and ran to our numbered spot. After the officers finished their daily check in we all headed down to the canteen for the Navy's version of breakfast; if you can call it that. Powdered eggs, sausages that I swear were left over from the civil war, and hockey pucks that I think at one time might have been toast. I tried to choke down what I could and thought I would find a dog to give the rest to, but then I thought, nah even a dog would be smarter then to eat this shit.

After slop fest we headed back to our number and waited for our daily assigned work detail. On that first day we noticed that our numbers were in the back of the line which would come in very handy as we were to soon find out. We each decided that we did not feel like working our first day on base so we all slowly made our way to the road behind us. We were all shocked that it worked. None of us were called for work detail that day.

Having the entire day off, we decided to explore the base together. It looked like a typical military base. The buildings looked like a good stiff wind would blow them over, but we were really surprised by how many of them there were. The base itself had to be at least a mile long and had everything from a bowling alley, to a movie house, officer clubs, as well as several canteens where you could buy candy bars, cigarettes, magazines, books and various food items. They even had the Navy's version of a post office.

Since our idea worked so well the day before, we decided to try our luck again and surprise surprise it did! We got out of work detail yet again. In fact none of us ever had work detail the entire time we were at Treasure Island.

After about a month we finally got our orders. I was given the rank of E3 assigned to an A.T.C. vessel. Don't know what that is? Neither did I, so my buddies and I decided to go to the base library to find out what exactly we were in for. I could not believe what I saw on the pages before me. The so-called boat was a 30 x 60foot hunk of metal that weighed 90 tons that had two Detroit diesel engines. The only thought that ran through my mind while looking at the images before me was "I am a dead man".

After we had our orders we were all allowed to go home on a month's leave. I could not wait to see my wife and family and to some good ole fashioned home cooking.

I remember getting off yet another commercial flight back in Milwaukee saying goodbye to my buddies and heading back home with my Dad. When I saw Phyllis for the first time we held each other so close that neither wanted to let go. That night I told Phyllis about the boat I was being assigned to and told her about how scared I was. She listened and told me not to worry, that everything would be all right.

Having nothing better to do, I decided the next day that I would go back to work for my uncle at Purdy Steaks. Phyllis was still working there and I really wanted to see her as much as possible before I had to leave again, and besides, money was very tight back then and we needed as much of it as we could get before I left.

When the day came that I had to go to Vallejo California to finish my basic training, I had this uneasy feeling that I would never see my family again. I told Phyllis that if something happened to me she should go on and forget about me. With a kiss and a hug I got back into my dad's car and once again headed for the airport. Again, we didn't say much but I knew deep down how he must have felt. He knew what I was heading for and there was nothing he could do to stop it. All he could do was to give me a ride to the airport. How I loved him for not making that departure any harder then it was. The one thing that was different this time was that my dad got out and gave me a hug. I grabbed my gear headed into the airport and never looked back.

CHAPTER 3

BASIC TRAINING

I again traveled on a commercial airline with the same group of guys that I went to Treasure Island with, but something was different this time. I guess knowing that playtime was over weighed heavily on everyone's mind. We all knew that this time we were going to learn how to be soldiers. We knew this training could mean the difference of whether you came home in one piece or not at all. I know for me it was a huge turning point. I didn't know what would lie ahead for me, but I knew that whatever life was going to bring me from this day forward would forever change me.

After a lot of inner sole searching on a long flight, we landed in San Francisco. We again took a shuttle bus but this time it was to a place called Mare Island in Vallejo, California. Mare Island was a decommissioned submarine base converted into a training facility for incoming Naval soldiers. The base had its similarities to Treasure Island in that it looked like a typical military base, but we soon found that it was very different.

Treasure Island was more of a pit stop along the way. But Mare Island, in 1969 anyway, had very few amenities. In fact the only building that was not used for military training purposes or sleeping quarters was a tiny makeshift bar that trainees could go to unwind. Once in a while there would be a band playing and, if you were lucky, the band might even be worth listening to. But, still, it was the only thing to do to get our minds off of what all this pain in the ass training was for.

For starters, all our trainers were Marine instructors that were Vietnam returnees. I was surprised at first to find out we were being trained by Marines and not Naval officers, but when our training was over and we got to Vietnam, we were all grateful for each and every one of those Marines. They knew exactly what we were headed for and what we would need to know to come back in one piece. They were in no way shape or form easy on us. In fact from the time we crawled out of bed to the time we fell back into them we had something going on. But when I got back from Vietnam I knew deep down that it was those marines more than anything else was that brought me home in one piece. And for that, from the bottom of my heart, I would like to thank them. One and all.

Our days at Mare Island started every morning at 0500 when we were thrown out of our beds and told you have 10 minutes to get your asses outside. We then ran anywhere from 3-5 miles depending on the mood of the marine instructor in charge of that particular day's activities. If anyone took longer then the time we were given to get going, we were guaranteed to run even further. Needless to say we learned real quick not to try the patience of our instructors.

After they finished running us we were able to get something that resembled food then were instructed on which training exercise we would be doing that day. Which could consist of anything from how to maneuver PBR's and ACT's, how to disassemble, reassemble and general maintenance on various weapons, hand to hand combat and basic war zone survival skills. Our instructors were hard on us and we hated them for it, but we knew, even then, that our coming back alive depended on how well we learned what they were teaching us. But still, it really sucked.

Well I can't say all of it sucked. We all liked training on the different naval vessels. Each one had its own unique features and we sure had fun learning them all. But I've got to say that my favorite was by far the PBR.

A PBR is a river patrol boat which is basically a converted fiberglass pleasure boat rebuilt to get soldiers in and out of combat areas as quickly as possible. They are powered by Jacuzzi jet pumps that allow them to not only achieve speeds of up to 25-29 knots almost instantaneously, but they are able to stop on a dime. Our first day on these vessels we were able to take turns getting it up to top speed, then our instructors would yell **STOP THE BOAT**. Man that was fun. We almost forgot why we were there.

Another type of boat we trained on was known as an armored troop carrier, otherwise known as an ATC. The ATC was more like the type of boat you imagine when you think of a military vessel. It is a 30 x 60-foot hunk of metal that weighs 90 tons. Obviously the ATC's are not nearly as quick as the PBR's but they had some unique features of their own. One being that the ATC's are sturdier and far larger than the PBR's which means you feel more secure on open waters. We would find out later that we were trained on both vessels because although different in structure, both ATC's and PBR's served similar purposes, but in different ways, and it would be good to know both so we could be reassigned to either if needed.

Although both vessels were used for everything from hauling troops and supplies to assisting other military branches with various missions, the PBRs were used mostly in open waters. Here their speeds were a great asset, while the ATC's were used more on the narrow rivers where their heavy metal frames provided more protection from the all too frequent friendly fire they were subjected to. And wouldn't you know it, I was assigned to an ATC known as the "Fickle Finger of Fate" but I will get more into that later.

After we got a handle of the vessels we would be stationed on, it was on to the next phase of our training; the basic maintenance of various weapons.

Not surprising, but the Marines were well versed on all the different weapons we would be using and they were not about to let us leave without knowing everything about every weapon. We were not only trained on what every weapon could do, but what it could not do as well. We learned how to disassemble and reassemble (M16s, M79s, M14s, M1s, 20 Mik Miks, 60 50 & 30) calibers, and various pistols. By the time we were done, we could take them all apart and reassemble them blindfolded.

Now that we knew how to maintain the weaponry, it was time to learn how to fire them. For that we were to spend a weekend at Camp Pendleton. I personally was really looking forward to this part of the training because I have always had a fascination with firearms for as long as I could remember. And although I was not exactly thrilled with why I was being trained on how to use them, it was still going to be interesting learning how to use them accurately. I was a little disappointed to find out we would only get two days for firing practice, but I guess we were needed so badly in Vietnam that they were rushing through our training as fast as possible. Don't get me wrong, we were trained very well, it was just more rapid then it would normally be.

The firing range at Camp Pendleton was nothing more then an open field with old tanks and jeeps scattered about that we were to use as targets. We took turns in groups of 10 or so shooting various weapons with our instructors by our side explaining how to shoot the weapon and giving advice on various adjustments we each had to make to increase our accuracy. I may have went into this training not being able to hit the broad side of a barn, but I left knowing I could shoot a tic off a dogs ear at 50 yards and never wake the dog from its nap.

Well now we knew how to operate the boats and we knew how to fire and maintain our weapons, but what if we were in a position where we could not use our weapons? What then? Answer: hand to hand combat.

Our instructors showed us how to disarm an attacker, how to counter react any aggressive move, and most of all, if all else fails, kick them in the nuts then do it again so they stay down. Then, once they're down, stomp on their ankles, crushing them as much as possible so they could not run and you could contain them. Next the instructors told us to inform the prisoner if he moved you would shoot him. If the guy chose to get up and run shoot him right then and there. Do not hesitate because if you do you are a dead man.

Now that we knew how to handle ourselves, and our equipment, it was time to put our skills to the test. For this we were to be flown to Washington State. I thought to myself, great a nice quiet flight, maybe a bag of peanuts along the way, YEAH RIGHT!

The type of plane we boarded was called a box car plane. And, just as the name suggests it is pretty much a flying box. If you were lucky you were able to sit on some of the straps that were attached to the walls. Otherwise you sat on the hard floor the entire turbulent way!!!

When the plane landed we were all glad to be back on the ground. That is until we found out what our up-coming week was going to entail.

We were lead to a wooded area that was miles from our intended location. We were then given parachutes, maps, and coordinates to our predetermined destination. When we asked where our food rations were we were told we would have to learn to live off the land.

After we had our gear, our instructors let us know that we had one day to make it to the coordinates they gave us and if by some miracle we made it back within that time we would be rewarded. Little did we know, or maybe deep down we did, that we were never meant to reach our destination.

We camped out that first night by turning our parachutes into makeshift tents. Now seeing how we were in an area that was consistently warm year round we were shocked when it snowed that night. We tried everything to keep warm. We even brought rocks and logs from the fires we had started into our tents but even that did little to ward off the bone chilling cold. Somehow we all made it through the night and started heading toward the coordinates we were given.

After we had been walking for several hours we were ambushed by our machine gun bearing instructors and lead to a re-incarnated Vietnamese prison camp complete with gate and tower guards, underground bunkers and 6 x 6-foot boxes with a ceiling no higher than 3feet.

We were first lead into the underground bunker and told to get some rest. Just as we found a way to arrange ourselves to make sleeping even remotely possible, our captures threw a smoke grenade in the bunker. Gasping for air, we tripped and clawed each other trying to make it out of the bunker. When we finally made it out we were thrown one by one into the 6foot boxes, given a password and told not to give up that password no matter what.

When it was my turn in the box, I was slapped to the ground then picked up thrown into a chair where I was then hit repeatedly just shy of any real damage but it sure felt like it was. But, through it all, I did not give up my password.

After a week of being slapped around, denied food and showers, and basically being totally dominated by our "captors," we were escorted to the local base where we were able to eat our first meal in a week. I've got to say; not eating for a week made even military food seem appetizing and I never thought that would be possible. The funny thing was that we smelled so bad after not showering for a week that we were able to sit wherever we wanted which was a privilege we were not often given.

After we chowed down we all filed again into our flying box and headed back to Mare Island. Now as bad as I thought the way to Washington was, being in that box with 50+ guys that have not showered in over a week made the trip to Mare Island down right unbearable.

When we got back to the Mare Island base and were able to finally get cleaned up, we hit the sack. Glad to actually be sleeping on our now much appreciated cots, each wondering what the hell these bastards had in store for us next.

I woke up the next morning thinking that after the hell they put us through last week our training had to be over with and that we would be packing up and heading for Vietnam. **WRONG!!!!!!** Our instructors had one more surprise for us.

For our last days of training we were told to board some old ATCs and head into the slues. With smartass grins on their faces they told us to be prepared for some "surprises" along the way, remember our training, and be prepared to defend yourselves. After all the hell they have put us through already, I knew nothing good could come from the way they said "Surprises." Besides they were much too happy to have that word not mean something.

Putting myself on guard I joined seven other men on one of the many A.T.C.'S docked on the outskirts of narrow channels our instructors called the slues. One by one we each navigated our way through the many twists and turns wondering just what we were in store for.

About 15 minutes had gone by when all hell broke loose and for a split second me and my fellow crewmembers froze. Then all at once our training kicked in and we picked up our weapons and started firing everything we had toward the banks of the slues.

To give you a taste of what this was like, imagine the loudest thunderstorm you've ever heard. The kind the makes a house and ground shake. The explosion that makes you instinctively want to run for cover. The panic that starts at your gut and makes you shake from fear. Now times that by 10 and then it is repeated again and again and again and all of a sudden you realize you're on a metal boat, in the water, with no place to run.

When we finally got through the first fire fight, we thought to ourselves, that was not so bad, and we all started to congratulate ourselves for a job well done; big mistake. The next thing we knew it started all over again, but this time it was even worse. Our first instinct was to duck but, again, our training overpowered that instinct, and again we gave them hell.

When we made it all the way through the slues we turned around and headed back. We all sat on guard and watched everywhere for the slightest movement. We started to relax as we got almost all the way back when we were attacked again.

Once we completed this lesson in hell we found out that our instructors were throwing m80's at us and we were firing only blanks. Our instructors let us know they were trying to give us as close a feel for how things were going to be in country (a term used by service men and women meaning in the line of fire) as they were able to give. Then someone asked the inevitable question: "Is that what it's really going to be like over there?" The Marines looked us over and said "not even close." They said there was no way of duplicating what we were going to be experiencing exactly, but that we had been given all the tools we would need to survive no matter what those bastards had to throw at us.

Then they sat us all down and gave us the best advice we had been given up to this point. Remember your training. When everything else goes wrong, REMEMBER YOUR TRAINING!!! And whatever you do, do not surrender. It is far better to die with dignity than to spend time as a prisoner of war. The week you spent in Washington was nothing compared to what will happen to you if you are a guest at the Hanoi Hilton (one of the more famous Vietnamese prison camps). Just keep your heads down, give them hell, and you'll come back home.

That was it. We made it through basics and it was time to put all this bullshit to use. I still was not quite sure what I was in for, but I knew that I had plenty of reasons to come home. With that in mind I sat down to write my last letter before heading overseas to my parents and another to Phyllis.

I knew what I wanted to say but when I sat down to put it into words I found myself staring at a blank piece of paper. After all, I didn't want to worry anyone. I had that part handled myself. Besides no matter what I wrote, I knew my family would be beside themselves until I was back safely in the states.

In the end I decided to keep my letters short and upbeat. I explained that I was being shipped out and that I would write again as soon as I could. I told them that I had the best training I could possibly have, I knew that God was watching out for me, and that I loved them all very much.

With an overwhelming sense of longing for home, I sealed the letters, slipped them into the mailbox, and headed for the barracks to pack my gear and spend my last night in the states.

I spent that time with the guys I have come to think of as my second family discussing what the chances were of all of us coming home. We all knew that the statistics showed one of three people sent to Vietnam would end up either killed or hurt in some way before their tour was over.

When I went to bed that night all I could think about was God help me…Vietnam here I come!!!!!!

CHAPTER 4

ARRIVING IN VIETNAM

The next morning the Mare Island graduating class #169 headed for Vietnam. Well most of us anyway. Some of the guys got so loaded the night before that they were forbidden to get on the flight. I was to find out that they were sent over with the next class a month later.

I was horrified to see the flying box again. Surely they were not going to make us sit on the floor for the entire trip over there? Sure enough that is exactly what we had to do. From California all the way to our first stop in Japan.

As we approached the airstrip we would be landing at in Japan, we were told that when the plane lands we were to file out into a room that was reserved for G.I.s only. Thankful for a chance to stretch my legs a little, I proceeded into this small room that became very crowded with not only our group, but a group of returning G.I.s as well. And wouldn't you know it, I recognized a guy I went to high school with. As our eyes met he made his way through the crowded room and shook my hand.

He asked me if I was coming or going. I told him I was going, what about him. He looked at me kind of funny and said he was on his way home. I asked him what it was like over there and he said hell on earth. He went on to tell me about another guy we went to high school with named Mike Tomick. They were in country together on a routine mission when Mike stepped on a land mine. Mike made it home as far as he knew, but he would be surprised if he wasn't missing at least one of his legs if not both. He then advised me to keep my head down and not to volunteer for anything weird.

After that a man came in and announced the plane was refueled and it was time to get back on board. I turned back to the guy I was talking to and simply said I was glad that he was heading home. He once again shook my hand, looked me in the eye, and wished me a very heartfelt good luck. As he headed back to the men he was talking to, and I headed for the piece of crap that would take me to hell, I could not get out of my mind what he told me about Mike.

The next time we landed, I found myself in Saigon. All I can say to describe what was before my eyes was total chaos. People were everywhere. Traffic going in every which direction with no rhyme or reason to it. I didn't know what to make of it.

We were told to board a make shift military bus that had wire mesh along the windows. Without air-conditioning, windows in vehicles did not make sense in Vietnam where the average temperature was 85 degrees with a humidity level of well over 100%. But what was the reason for the wire mesh? When someone made a joke about it, we were told it was used to prevent the Vietcong from throwing grenades or other weapons into the bus. Welcome to hell, Mark.

When the bus stopped we found ourselves outside a military facility that I guessed at one time might have been used as a hotel. It was surrounded by service men with machine guns and had barbed wire from one end of it to the other. After we were given explicit instructions not to leave the building until it was time for us to leave, we headed up some well worn and precarious stairs for what we knew would be the first of many restless night sleep.

When we got up the next morning, we gathered our gear, which now contained a m16 rifle, and headed downstairs where we, once again, boarded the make shift bus.

After boarding, someone mentioned a conversation they overheard about a VC, short for Vietcong, that had come riding by our building on a scooter that night holding a very crude delayed bomb rigged with a remote timer. From what I understood, the VC tried to drop the homemade device when he was spotted by one of the guards. The guard convinced the VC he made the wrong choice by giving him an unforgettable gift from Uncle Sam; a bullet to the back of the head. We all rode the rest of the way back to the airport chatting about how if a place that guarded could be targeted, what were we in for out in the middle of nowhere.

When we were back in the air, we were in for some more good news from our pilot. He explained that we would probably be under fire when we approached our landing sight so he would be shutting off the engines when we got close.

He would then let the plane glide for a while in hopes to keep our landing as undetectable as possible.

We were instructed to start filing out of the plane while it was still taxing down the strip, which turned out to be nothing more than an open field, so the plane would be back in the air as quick as possible. Hopefully this might prevent the Vietnamese from taking out the plane, as well as giving away the fact that troops were dropped off. If not, the moment we landed we would be under immediate enemy fire with no place to hide.

After jumping out of the still moving plane, we high tailed it onto a truck where we were escorted further into Dong Tam. When we reached the end of the line, we found ourselves at a make shift military base somewhere along the Mekong Delta. We were each assigned to a hooch, which is a fancy word for an approximate 60 x 30 foot building designed for housing military personnel. It was at this point that me and my buddies from Mare Island were separated. It was then, for the first time, I felt really alone.

After quick good lucks and see ya laters I headed for my hooch to settle in for the night. As I lay there on my cot I started thinking about home. I wondered what Phyllis was doing and thought about our last night together. I drifted off remembering how she smelled so sweet, and felt so warm lying next me. I realized then and there how much I truly loved her, how lucky I was to have found her, and what a strong person she must be to stand faithfully behind me while I served my civic duty.

I had just drifted off to sleep when an explosion followed by the loudest siren I ever heard threw me to my feet. I instinctively ran for the opening of the hooch when I saw what seemed to be the end of the world happening right before my eyes. I was brought back to reality when I heard shouts coming from every direction to get down.

I started running for all I was worth to a pile of sandbags with a tin roof laid across the top which I later found out was called a bunker. The bunker was 4feet from another hooch and it seemed the safest place to be. When I got there I recognized Maize, one of the guys I met at Mare Island. When we both saw the bunker was full we looked around for somewhere else to go. Maize was transfixed by the explosive sounds coming from one of our helicopters mini guns and from the ammo dump being blown to pieces by enemy fire, while I went around to the side of the bunker and prayed I would come out of this alive.

I had gotten a mere 8 steps, when a round went off right where Maize and I had been standing not seconds before. The percussion blast threw me back at least ten feet landing me on my ass. I tried to get up but one of the walls of the hooch next to the bunker had fallen on top of me. I tried to pull the crap off but realized it was no use, I was trapped. While lying there screaming for help I did a quick check for all my body parts. Glad for the pain because I figured if it hurt, at least it meant it was still there.

I continued screaming like hell when I suddenly realized my voice was not the only one screaming. Someone else was in the same predicament I was in. After what seemed like hours, but probably was more like minutes, I felt the debris being lifted off me and found that I was finally able to crawl out.

Although I could still hear the shelling going off at the ammo dump, it was far enough away that I felt I could take a minute to come to grips with what just happened. It was then that I found him.

It was Maize. He had a hole in his side that I later found out was a result of the mere impact of the round that entrapped me. A medic was treating him and all I could do was just stare; I knew right then and there that he was dead.

I knew there was nothing I could do. I had to go on. I walked around in a state of shock. There were men laying all around being treated for various injuries screaming for help. Horrified by the scene laid out in front me, I barely noticed when another one of my Mare Island buddies had come running up to me. He started yelling something about Mike Bouballs, yet another one of our buddies from Mare Island. (I'm not sure of the spelling of the names so I would like to apologize to my buddies if I spelled them wrong). He told me that Mike's hooch was hit and he didn't know if Mike was still inside. We both ran to the pile of rubble that had once been Mike's hooch. The walls had given way and the ceiling had come crashing down. Thinking the worst I crawled through the mangled mess and found the guy that I knew had the bunk right below Mike.

Even though a blanket had been laid across him, I noticed a bloody arm dangling from beneath the blanket with a piece of shrapnel wrapped around it. Sickened by the sight I made my way back through the rubble announcing my findings to my awaiting buddy.

We managed to flag down an MP that told us Mike had sustained a shattered jaw and was missing part of his lower lip so they evacuated him by chopper to a nearby hospital where he would be fixed up then eventually sent home.

I thought to myself "Thank God." "At least he is done with all this crap." I told my buddy that I was going back to my hooch to see what was left of it and he said he was going to do the same. As I made my way through what was left of the base, I let my mind wander over the events of the past couple of hours.

First Maize, now Mike, and this was only our second day here? How in the hell does anyone survive this? Why them? Why did I survive relatively unharmed while all these men around me didn't? I couldn't take the guilt I was feeling. All I wanted to do was to go to my hooch, lay down and never get up.

When I finally got back to what I thought was my hooch, I was in for yet another surprise. The hooch I was in not two hours before must have been hit by motor fire because it was in shreds, and along with it, my cot and all my gear. So here I was in an active war zone, one of my buddies dead, another injured. I had no clothes, no gear, and no place to sleep. And just think, you only have 13 months to go Purdy.

Well at least we won't be bombed again for a while. Or at least that is what I thought. The next day Charlie, a word we used for the N.V. and their allies, was at it again. This time they didn't do as much damage, but the noise was deafening. How could anyone get used to this?

One of the guys in the hooch I was reassigned to explained that Charlie was nothing if not persistent. Trying to hide my shock and amazement I simply asked him what I should do about my blown up gear. He explained that the M.P.s had some forms for replacing it so I headed off with at least a little hope for some good news.

Eventually, after 5 days and nights of Charlie reminding us of their presence, I was told by a captain of one of the 25 A.T.C. boats to grab my gear. When I just started to follow him with nothing in my hand he looked at me like "Uh.. your gear" I explained how I didn't have any thanks to Charlie. He chuckled and said, "well that just sucks doesn't it." I shrugged my shoulders and said lead the way.

The captain brought me to a bunch of A.T.C. boats harbored in a small cannel on the Macon Delta, which he explained, is a river that branches out over much of Vietnam and is used by the North to supply its troops. When we got to his boat he said welcome aboard to the Riv Ron 13 platoons boat #12.

These A.T.C.s were similar to the ones we learned on at Mare Island but this one had a chopper pad on the front of it. Actually, I was surprised at how small the chopper pad actually was. In fact, I was to find out that the only way a chopper could land on it at all was sideways.

We climbed aboard and he lead me to the starboard (right) side of the boat to a round circle of steel with a 20 mm anti aircraft gun sticking out of it. He half jokingly said welcome to your new best friend and invited me to check it out. I climbed in the cramped space and started making mental notes of how I could make the area more user friendly. After I was done surveying the claustrophobic area, the captain took me below deck where the crew slept and stored their gear.

There were cots stacked along the floor in various positions. Some would be side by side but others were stacked one on top of the other resembling make shift bunk beds. The crews' gear was thrown on a wooden shelf just under the rafters of the ships' hull. This was done in hopes of keeping the rats, snakes and other unwelcome quests from getting to them. Given the circumstances, it did seem to make the most sense.

Just above the hull was a storage bin that held the ships essentials from minor repair parts to ropes used for anchoring san pans while the crew inspected their cargo. But more importantly it was here that the delicious sea rations were stored.

Ah sea rations. The pre 1950's cartons containing crackers, that disintegrated in your hand, and peanut butter and jelly, that if you were lucky you might be able to get a little out of the can. In all fairness some of the canned fruit wasn't so bad, and if you mixed the peanut butter, jelly and crackers together you could eat them with a spoon.

Some of the other sea rations contained candy bars that to this day I don't know what was in them. All I know was that I could not even chew them let alone swallow one. Others contained gum, which I did actually like. There was beef stew, powdered eggs, and other various dried foods that could best be described as the ramen noodles of today but only after they have been sitting around for 25 + years. Some sea rations even contained cigarettes.

After the captain finished his tour, I decided to sum up the boat on my own. One of the first things I noticed was that I did not like the layout of the cots. There was little air down in the hull, not to mention thoughts of snakes and rats crawling on me were more than a little alarming. Also, if there were any reasons, which I was sure there would be, to get to my gun, it would mean tripping over other cots and gear adding seconds that I am sure would cost lives.

I thought for a minute how to fix this and was struck by an ingenious idea. I asked the captain if I could return to the base for a few minutes and although he was puzzled by my request he said go for it. When I came back an hour later he looked completely shocked to see what I had gone back for. It was a medical stretcher that I knew was never used and some rope that I found lying around.

I took the rope and threw it over the middle of some rafters on the top of the well deck. I then secured the stretcher so it hung down about three feet from the top. It was great. I was able to get any breeze that might come along at night, and I was able to jump from one side of the boat to the other in a split second. But most of all, it lightened my worries about the snakes and rats. The captain and my shipmates came down to see what I was up to, took one look at what I had done, and laughed their asses off.

Since I had no gear to store, I followed my new shipmates up top where I spent most of the night getting to know the crew.

The guys started riding me about my hanging bunk idea and jokingly asked where I hid my gear suggesting some rather crude places. I made a callous joke about Charlie, feeling I didn't need to be burdened down with such luxuries like clothes and they all laughed again. When I explained that I filled out the paperwork for replacements they stopped laughing and told me that I might see my gear when I was back in the states if I was lucky. I was better off going through the black market, which turned out to be the best advice I had been given over there.

I would come to find out that the black market was a great place for getting whatever you needed. It was certainly faster then waiting on the Navy. They had everything from clothes, to food, to luxury items like radios and cameras. With the help of my shipmates, I learned that sea rations were as good as gold to the Vietnam black market. It seems, as much as we hated our sea rations, the Vietnamese couldn't get enough of them. And as far as we were concerned, they could have them. Anyway, A month later I had managed to at least replace some of the gear I had lost.

Now before anyone thinks anything bad about this, let me explain that I was without clothes for almost a month before I turned to the black market. It was another two months after that before the Navy sent me anything, and that was only because my mother was astute enough to call Senator Proxmire of Wisconsin. He got the ball rolling for me and was able to get replacements for all the gear I had lost. Thanks Mom.

CHAPTER 5

LIFE AS A RIVER RAT

I spent that first night tucked up in my hanging sanctuary with the sounds of the water gently passing by the ship. I couldn't help but wonder what would happen if the boat were suddenly attacked. Would I be able to get out? Would that even be the right thing to do? If I did get out where would I go, back to the base camp maybe? Yeah Mark, they never attack anyone there. But seriously, where would I go. I fell asleep contemplating what the best move would be.

After yet another restless night sleep I got up and started heading up top. It was already hot and humid so I decided to forget the only shirt I had and, thinking I would not need pants again for quite some time, I cut up my only pair of greens into something resembling shorts.

On my way up top one of the guys stopped me and said to wait a minute. When I asked why my answer came in the way of a 5-6 foot headless black snake dangling from the end of a machete. As I fell down three steps the guy just laughed and said they hadn't finished their pest control for the morning. **PEST CONTROL!!!!!!!** I shouted up, "that's what you call pest control?"

When I was told it was ok to come up I noticed the guy with the snake-dangling machete was chopping off the head of yet another rather large "Pest". I was told that the Snakes came on board every morning to get some heat from the metal decks. They showed me how to take a stick, hold down the head and whack it off with the tip of the machete. Then take the head and the rest of the snake and toss it overboard as quickly as possible.

Now as surprising as this seems, I never once asked if these snakes were poisonous. In fact, I didn't find out until my wife and I started writing this book that only three of the many many many variety of snakes were not deathly poisonous. To this day I don't know what kind of snakes these were. All I know is they were brown or black and they were usually at least 5-6 feet long.

Once the pest control had been completed, the crew each grabbed a box of sea rations and started choking down breakfast. If you've never had powdered eggs before there is just no way to describe the taste. For me, personally, I would have rather eaten the box it came in. So I usually settled for the sea rations with canned pears and peanut butter and jelly with crackers.

After breakfast I had to do my morning ritual and asked someone where exactly this was done. Everyone had a little chuckle but one of the guys said "Why the Navy has spared no expense and supplied us with all the modern conveniences aboard this here vessel." He proceeded to take me to the stern (back) of the ship and pointed out a 5-gallon paint bucket with a rope attached to its handle. He handed it to me, smacked me on the back and said "Don't forget to Flush."

I lowered the bucket just enough to fill it ¼ of the way and looked around for the most secluded spot I could find. When I finished cleaning the bucket out I put it back in its designated location and proceeded to find the rest of the crew.

After everyone had finished up whatever they had to do, the captain called us all together and passed along that our mission for the day was mine patrol. The guys all headed to the stern of the ship and flipped the switches that released the 7foot chains into the river. We then cast off and I was heading down the Mekong Delta for the first time and out into the open waters to protect one of the anchored repair vessels.

I was surprised to see how narrow the Mekong Delta actually was. In some places it couldn't be more than 50 yards wide, yet in others it could be more than a mile. But no matter where you went the water was so murky and brown that seeing anything underwater was impossible.

After we finished throwing the chains overboard I headed to my gun mount. I loaded the ammo and looked up and down the shoreline for any movement and psychologically prepared myself for the possibility of taking another human life. How did I get to this point? Could I actually take a human life? What if I froze at the wrong time? What if the gun jams? What if they kill me before I can fire my first shot? What if I miss?

All the training in the world never prepares you for shooting at another person. I am a child of the Lord. I was raised to respect the rights and feelings of others, not to destroy them. I suddenly found myself praying. Not only for myself, but for a country being torn apart by war. I prayed that He would give me strength to do what I had to do and forgive me for whatever sins I had to commit to come out of this alive.

I tried to remind myself just why we were here. Surely there had to be a better reason than killing people that, from what I could see, didn't have much to fight for anyway. And why was this war taking so long? The Americans had all the modern warfare equipment money could buy. Surely we could take this ill-equipped country with our eyes closed.

Athough this was very true, I learned not to underestimate the V.C. We may have had better equipment, but the V.C. were very good at building bombs out of just about anything they could get their hands on. For example, one of their favorite concoctions for the water was to take a ¼ metal drum, fill it with gunpowder, seal it with some kind of liquid, then attach a wire for a fuse that would run all the way to the nearest shore line. They finished it up by attaching orange inner tubes to it which allowed the barrel to float just below the waters surface making it impossible to see.

The V.C., who by the way are excellent swimmers, would swim with these barrels down stream out to one of our parked vessels, allowing the fuse line to drag along behind them. The V.C. would then find a way to anchor the make shift bomb to the boat. I am not sure exactly how they did this but if I had to hazard a guess I would say they tied them to the ships anchor lines. After the bomb was in place and the swimmer was far enough away, one of their comrades hidden along the shoreline would trigger the bomb.

This is where the chains came in. The chains had something resembling barbed wire intertwined in it so when we would drag the chains behind the boat the fuse lines of these contraptions would get tangled and break away from the bombs making them useless.

Knowing the V.C. could slip in and out without being detected we would take as many preventive measures as we could. One of these measures was to throw percussion grenades, the equivalent of 2½ sticks of dynamite, into the river every ½ hour which had the power to kill anything in the water for at least 100 yards. This was so effective that it was not unusual for us to churn up V.C. bodies the morning after our mine deterrent runs.

Surprisingly enough, despite all our efforts, some of our A.T.C.s did fall victim to these V.C. contraptions. In fact, I just happened to see a ship shortly after it had been struck. The crew informed us that the ship was lifted at least 10 feet in the air then landed upside down in the water; no small feat for a 90-ton hunk of metal. The crew had survived, thank God, with just some scrapes and bruises, but I guess others, prior and since, were not so lucky.

Minesweeping usually meant a 12-24 hour shift. This one was no different. After we had finally finished our mission we headed back to our channel for some sleep and to await our next orders. I was glad that my first mission went so smoothly and could only hope that the rest would be so good.

By this time I had come to the conclusion that a good night sleep would not happen again until I was safe at home with my beloved Phyllis. Whenever we had down time I could not help but let my mind drift back to what my life was like before I came to this indescribable mind altering prison of hopelessness. I would wonder what my life was going to be like when, or should I say if, I ever got home.

The mornings for a River Rat brought to me some mixed emotions. First it meant that I survived another night of Charlie's bullshit, and second I still had, at this point anyway, 12+ months to go. But what I did notice by the second week in country, was that I started falling into a mindset of survival of the fittest. By this I mean that I started figuring out that if I was going to be able to come out of this in one piece with as little psychological damage as humanly possible, that I was going to have to come to terms with what war was. I had to do what I had to do. I didn't have to like it, but I did have to accept that this was going to be my life for 13 months.

With that in mind, I started each day with a prayer for my safety, and a determination to get through this no matter what it took.

I got up the morning after the minesweeping detail wondering what our next detail would bring. I was to learn that the captains of all the A.T.C's would get together at the end of each detail, which could be anywhere from once a week to once a day, and discuss which ship would be assigned to which duty. As it turns out my ships next duty was patrolling the Mekong Delta.

Patrolling the Delta meant we were to drive up and down the Delta pulling over any sampans that we thought looked suspicious. Especially those sampans heading for V.C. Island.

V.C. Island was a small patch of land, located just across the Delta from where my home base was. It was infested with blood hungry V.C. just looking for an opportunity to wipe out as many Americans and their allies as they could.

One of the more popular weapons used from the island were rocket launchers made from bamboo poles with flags attached to the end. The flags were there to improve the accuracy of the rockets but it also helped us spot them. Now granted you literally had to be looking almost right at them to see them, and most of the time the V.C. had gotten off at least one or two rounds before you spotted them, but once you did you knew just where to fire.

Now the general rule of thumb was that you did not fire just because you saw the poles because you didn't want to waste valuable ammo. Instead it meant that you had your weapon aimed at the spot and you looked for any kind of movement in that general area.

It may seem foolish to not just fire anyway whenever a pole was spotted, but once a pole was used, it was not uncommon for the V.C. to just leave it still in the firing position. Also, the Island had more then just V.C. on it.

V.C. Island was also the home of several local villages inhabited with innocent women and children, which the V.C. had learned to use to their advantage. The V.C. would overcome these villages, and line up the women and children in front of their troops along the banks of the river. This way when you were firing at what you thought were just V.C.

troupes, you also knew you were firing at innocent women and children as well.

This particular day started off as uneventful as the one before. We simply untied from the rest of the A.T.C.s got into our perspective places and started heading down the Delta. It didn't take us long before the captain spotted a suspicious looking sampan that he wanted to investigate.

The process for pulling over a sampan was relatively simple. We would motion the sampan operator over by calling out "la de" which means come hear in Vietnamese. Usually, the sampan would make its way over to us where we would tie it up to our boat so that we could board it and check their cargo. Keeping two guns pointed at the occupants of the sampan at all times.

Since we had no way of knowing if the sampan was local traffic or V.C. sympathizers, we had to maintain the same pattern no matter what. The local traffickers must have been used to this scenario because they didn't seem to be overly upset by our presence.

The standard procedure for boarding a sampan was to have one guy get on the front, another on the back, while a third inspected the cargo.

I learned early on to never inspect a sampan's cargo by lifting up lids or putting my hands into rice pots. The custom was to check all rice containers with a stick. If this turned up any hidden cargo like liquor or weapons, the container was dumped onto the floor of the sampan. We would then have them lift lids to any and all crates. This lessened the chance for injury due to any surprise booby-traps hidden throughout the cargo. Once the cargo was inspected the occupants would be asked to hand over their paperwork.

No matter who was in the sampan they had to have some kind of paperwork explaining what they were doing on the Delta. The papers were written in Vietnamese but after a while you got used to looking for certain similarities that were on legitimate traveler's paperwork. If their papers were legit, we would have them on their way again within minutes.

If not we would confiscate the cargo then pull the sampan to the nearest interrogation facility. Here they would determine exactly what the occupant's intentions were. If they were indeed working with the V.C. the occupants would be taken to the nearest prison facility. If it turns out they were just locals out on the Delta they would be released and their cargo was returned to them.

To keep good relations going we tried to offer innocent travelers gifts of sea rations, or treats for the children on board. Anything we had extra was appreciated. These small gestures might seem trivial, but by starting and maintaining good relations with the locals it made our job a lot easier.

All in all, the locals that were using the river for legitimate reasons were usually happy to comply with our intrusions. After all they knew we were there to protect their interest and the gifts they got more than made up for being inconvenienced for a few minutes.

The problems came when the sampan operators did not stop when asked. In these situations we had to fire a warning shot just ahead of the sampan. If they came over we kept our guns on them, boarded the boat and did a more thorough search.

If they made the foolish choice of ignoring our warning shots; we would take aim and destroy the sampan and everyone on it. We could not take the chance of boarding these sampans because more than likely they would be V.C. sympathizers and would think nothing of taking out as many of us as they could.

As luck would have it, my first time patrolling was as uneventful as my first minesweeping duty was. However, my next mission was to put me and my training to the ultimate test.

CHAPTER 6

LESSONS IN WARFARE

I would like to take a minute and warn you that this chapter is about the realities of war. This chapter will be very graphic in nature and does put some service men in a very bad light.

I struggled with my conscience for a long time about weather or not I should even include these events in this book. In the end, I decided that I want to keep this book as accurate as possible and to do that, I can't eliminate the bad aspects of war just because it puts Americans in a bad light. The truth is war is what it is. To eliminate the reality of it does an injustice to those service men who never made it home.

I would also like to explain that the service men I am talking about have seen things the V.C. have done that would sicken the strongest of souls. I in no way, shape or form blame them for their actions. I have seen only sporadic pieces of what they had to face on a daily basis. Things no one should ever have to see. If you have never been in a war zone like Vietnam, then understand that when you see the things these men have seen, it takes all sense of compassion out of you. Especially for people who can show such total disregard for not only their enemies, but for innocent children of their own people whose only misfortune was to be born in a country enplagued by war.

That having been said if you don't want to read the graphic details of this chapter, skip to chapter 7. If not please read on with an open mind and walk away with a new understanding of how much hell war really is.

Over the next few days we took turns with the other A.T.C.s patrolling the Delta. Then one day our captain announced we had received alternate orders.

This particular day we had been told we were to go with another service unit (to protect the ones involved, I will not mention their branch of service) to a place nicknamed Greasy Cove located about 3 clicks from the ocean. Their mission was to go ashore and check out reports of a newly constructed V.C. village. Ours was to watch their boat and supply back up if needed.

Before going ashore the men checked their weapons and then fired each one once to verify they were working properly. When they felt confident that all their equipment was in optimal working order they headed ashore, but not before instructing us to stay with the boat no matter what happened.

After the service men had been gone about an hour, all hell broke loose. I could suddenly hear the sound of rapid gunfire followed by the unmistakable whine of rockets being launched into an area not 100 yards away from where we were docked. The sky had instantaneously filled with a thick all encumbering black smoke replaced seconds later with the bright orange and red glows that come only after the deafening sound of rockets hitting their intended mark.

Not knowing exactly where our troops were, we had no choice but to helplessly wait, starring at the spot they entered hoping they would be coming out soon. I started running for my gun mount when a voice came blasting over the radio shouting something covered up by the surrounding gunfire.

I grabbed the mike and asked them to repeat the message, which was answered by one of the service men screaming for us to start firing in their direction but to aim high over their heads. I jumped on my gun, aimed it as high as I dared, and fired everything I had just over the spot the service men entered.

The next thing I knew the men had come out running full speed while simultaneously firing their weapons behind them. All, that is, except one.

This guy was carrying two highly trained North Vietnamese mercenaries known as N.V.A. one under each arm. He must have just grabbed them and ran because neither one of the N.V.A. were bound in any way.

Now these guys have a pretty good idea of what's coming, so they're not going to just lay there and let this guy take them. They are kicking and clawing and biting at whatever part of this guy they can get to, doing whatever they had to do to this guy to let them go. And on top of that, this guy has more N.V.A. coming behind him firing everything they have at him, so he can't just take his time. He has to keep a hold of his prisoners while running through the jungle.

After all the N.V.A. are the most trained of all the N.V. They are not going to make their camp on the side of an open road, or build a clear trail with signs saying N.V.A. this way. They are about a mile deep in a very thick jungle. Thick tree branches everywhere, brush slicing up his skin just as much as the N.V.A. were, and underbrush on the ground entangling his feet more and more with each step.

Yet, here he comes ignoring whatever the N.V.A. and the jungle are doing to him. running full speed, having no problem keeping up with the rest of his platoon.

I couldn't believe it when he came out of the jungle and threw both of the prisoners on the bow of our boat. Then, quick as a flash, he grabbed one of the prisoners and yanked his arms behind him tying them together at the elbows. A split second later he did the same to the other one. He then forced them on their knees on the edge of our boat facing him, cocked his handgun, and took turns pointing it at each one of their heads.

He decided to interrogate them right then and there, which made me a bit nervous for two reasons. One was that the N.V.A. had been firing at us not minutes before. And two, I was not exactly sure what these service men were going to do. It turns out I had reasons to be worried.

The B.G. (big guy) took one of the N.V.A. and started talking to him fluently in Vietnamese. The N.V.A. just shook his head no from time to time obviously unwilling to tell the B.G. what he wanted to know. After 10 minutes of getting nowhere the B.G. pointed his gun at the N.V.A.'s face and pulled the trigger.

The bullet entered the middle of the N.V.A.'s forehead and sent a spray of blood and brain matter streaming down the river before he fell into the murky river never to come up again. Then, without blinking an eye, the B.G. turned to the other prisoner and pointed his gun at his head. Then, with his other hand, he pointed to the spot where the N.V.A. went into the river and said something to him in Vietnamese.

I was to find out later that the men whose unfortunate job it was to interrogate prisoners found that if they tortured one prisoner in front of another, the second prisoner would then be more likely ready to cooperate.

This must have been the case here because when the B.G. started asking this prisoner what I could only guess were the same questions as before, he was much more successful. The second prisoner, unable to hide the terror in his eyes, started talking very rapidly, and in great detail, after each of the B.G.'s questions.

After several minutes of interrogation, the B.G. must have figured he had gotten all the information out of his prisoner that he was going to get. So, without removing his stone cold gaze from the quivering N.V.A. kneeling before him, he asked his fellow comrades what they wanted him to do with the gook.

He started suggesting they turn him over to the prison camp nearby, but then something happened that I would never forget as long as I live.

At first most of the B.G.'s battalion agreed with the idea of bringing the prisoner to the prison camp. That is until one of them pointed out that their unit was planing their monthly steak and beer party later that night. Another man went on to complain that if they brought the prisoner in they would be spending hours filling out paperwork and might miss out on their share of the festivities and no gook was worth that.

The B.G., still refusing to release his compassionless gaze from the terrified man cowering on his knees before him, addressed the platoon in general asking what they wanted him to do. In the end, they all agreed that no gook was worth losing any sleep over, so the B.G. shrugged his shoulders and said all right.

The prisoner must have figured out what everything meant because he suddenly let out the most horrific scream I ever heard. To be silenced only when the bullet went through his brain again sending a stream of red down river followed by a sickening splash as he hit the water.

I thought the first time I would see someone kill another human being I would feel something. But instead I just chalked it up to "this is war." If this sounds cold, then you need to understand that these men had a job to do. This wasn't a cop bringing down a drug dealer. These were two men that had they been given the chance, would have killed each and every one of us without giving it a second thought. It was them or us, and I for one was determined to go home in one piece no matter what it took.

The service men gathered their gear then jumped back onto their own boat. After making a few minor housekeeping adjustments, they gave us a mock salute, said thanks for the help, and headed back up the Delta and onto their festivities.

After we stowed away our own gear, we too headed back up the Delta to our own base. Not to a welcoming steak and beer dinner mind you, but after all that just happened we were just glad to be in one piece.

The next day we continued on with our routine sampan checks. This would go on for about two to three weeks. Occasionally we had to transport troops up or down the Delta helping out where ever and whoever required our services. But relatively speaking this was a pretty quiet time for us. Sure the V.C. would continue their two and three minute bursts of aggression, but all in all it was nothing out of the ordinary until one horrible horrible day.

My boat had been on a routine surveillance of the shores of the Delta when I heard the captain say awh hell **OPEN FIRE!!!!!!!!!**

My instincts kicked in and I just started swinging my 20mm anti aircraft gun up and down the shoreline. All I could see was smoke and trees being sliced in half by the force of my ammo. I just continued to fire until the captain called for the all clear.

The captain then got on the radio and called for a head count. I was trying to regain the hearing in my ears from the thundering noise of my gun, when the captain came up to me and said to reload my gun and stand ready because he didn't think this was over with yet.

Little did I know how true this was. The captain said look sharp boys and then it hit. We had just turned around the bend when we were under extreme firepower from the banks of the river.

We were so close to the shore on both sides that the V.C. had no trouble hitting their marks. I was in my gun mount giving the bastards everything I had when as suddenly as it started the shelling stopped.

It was deathly quiet until the boat that was trailing us came around the same bend and they too were put under the fury of the V.C. I looked back and started to turn my gun around to try and help them out when I noticed something was very wrong.

The boat had been bouncing from shore to shore. It would crash hard on one shore then head for the next crashing again sending us on a dangerous ride that could end up with V.C. jumping on and taking over our boat.

I hollered at the guy in the other gun mount to grab the wheel and open this damn thing up full speed until we get the hell out of here.

As quick as I could I climbed out of my gun mount and started running through the ship when I found one of the crew down in the hull of the boat with a shrapnel wound in his leg. I sat him up along the side of the boat and wrapped his leg the best I could.

After tending to him I began my search once more. It only took me a minute to come across another crewmember that had a much more serious injury to his crotch and butt. He was lying in a pile of blood and had pieces of bone and flesh hanging out of the hole in his crotch.

I picked him up and put him in the only bed still in one piece, the captains. I asked what I could do for him and he said he knew he was done and asked if I would just give him two shots of morphine to kill the pain.

I found the tubes of morphine that we had on board, attached the needle, shoved it in his arm and squeezed the contents of the tube into his arm the best I could. I then honored his request and gave him the second dose. As I was administering the morphine to him he explained that a motor round had entered the boat and hit the wall behind him sending shrapnel at him in every which direction. After I completed shoving the second tube in his arm he had succumbed to the pain. He was gone within minutes.

I left him lying in the captain's bed and headed back to the helm of the ship. Here I found the captain of the boat with a shrapnel wound to his face. The other gunner had already helped him and then pointed to the driver of the boat who had been killed instantly by motor fire. Knowing there was nothing I could do for him I simply put a towel over his head and proceeded to take the wheel from the other gunner.

I told him to get on the radio and call for a medivac while I got us out of there. Within minutes we had a medivac chopper on our landing pad.

After the chopper left, me and the other gunner took a minute to gather in all that had just happened. Between the two firefights and losing most of our crew in a matter of minutes I was spent. With no captain or crew we decided to head back to our base camp.

After we had tied up the boat, I decided to go below deck and see what I could salvage. I was shocked to see my hanging cot had come through all that hell with surprisingly little damage. I climbed onto my cot and just laid there staring up at the ceiling trying to put everything that just happened into perspective. Sleep was out of the question so I went to the only place that I knew would give me a sense of peace, home.

I let my mind drift back to what my life was like before Uncle Sam came calling. Mom's home cooking, Dad's gentle guiding light through all my ups and downs, my younger brothers doing their thing, hanging out with my buddies without some gook trying to pick us off, but most of all Phyllis. Just thinking about her set my mind back into a more focused place. In fact, now that I think back, if it weren't for those brief moments of recharging my minds batteries I don't think I would have come out of all that hell as well as I did.

Don't get me wrong, everyone that experiences the realities of war first hand comes out of it with their own battle scars, myself included. I just mean I was eventually, in time, able to put most of the war behind me when I got home. But more on that later.

The other gunner and I spent that night in silence. Neither one of us wanted to relive what had happened, and we both needed time to deal with whatever demons we had rolling around in our heads. In fact I'm not real sure what he did that night. All I knew was that I was glad that he was there. Even if I could not see him, knowing that someone else that had experienced the same thing that I did, was going through the same pain I was, just helped in some brotherhood sort of way.

The next day Lieutenant Kelly, our commanding officer, came on board our boat to inspect the damage the V.C. had done. He took an inventory of the supplies we would need and casually strolled through the boat like it was just another day. I can not tell you how much this pissed us off. We had just lost four of our crewmembers right before our eyes, and we were supposed to what, pretend this never happened? That, to us, was a disgrace.

After he had finished up his inspection, Lieutenant Kelly called us both over to him and told us to have a seat. Expecting an encouraging "you all did a great job, war is hell, are you both ok" speech, I was pissed beyond belief at his nonchalant attitude over the whole thing. Especially when he simply told us that we were going to be sent the supplies that we needed to replenish our boat, including 4 new recruits that would be there by the end of the week. What? Are human beings simply supplies now? Who needs a name anyway?

The truth is, in a war zone, men and women are supplies. At least to the higher ups anyway. I guess that was another reason why I felt writing this book was so important. I want to return my Fellow River Rats back into human beings, not just the forgotten numbers of a wartime battalion that no one mentions. We deserve better than that.

When Lt. Kelly had finished his replenishing spiel, he began his debriefing of the previous day's events. And if I thought his callousness of our slaughtered crew was bad, it was nothing compared to what he had to say next.

Lt. Kelly explained that after we had gotten back, a body assessment was conducted in the area where we were attacked. He, again with his nonchalant tone, said that on the side I was shooting on, I had wiped out a number of N.V.A. For a brief moment, I was almost glad. I started thinking that at least my crewmembers didn't die in vain. I managed to kill some of those sons of bitches. With a cold voice that sounded like somebody else speaking, I managed to spit out how many?!

Lt. Kelly explained that there was no way of knowing. He explained that there were several blood trails found, but the amount of blood on the ground indicated that more than one body was pulled for each trail making it impossible to even guess how many actual kills I had managed.

Lt. Kelly then said something I will never forget. In fact the memory still chills me to this day. He explained that before they ambushed us, the N.V.A. had lined up all the women and children from one of the local villages in front of their battalion. Along with the N.V.A., I had managed to kill seven women and 1 child. But worst of all, in the arms of one of the women, was a baby.

What kind of animals are these people? How could they be so... so... there are no words horrible enough to even describe these monsters. Even the worst animals on earth protect their young. These people use them for shields.

Sometime later I was to find out something else about the Vietnamese traditions that would further enhance my rage for the N.V.A. It seems that the Vietnamese people, at that time anyway, believed that for a soul to be at peace it had not only to be buried, but it had to be buried with all of its parts in one place. This meant that when the N.V.A. left the locals lying there, they hoped to not only take their lives, but to torture their eternal soles as well.

Being a man of God, I think the intentional unrest of souls was harder to handle than anything else. Our bodies are temporary, but our souls, our souls belong to God. How can this be going on?

Just when I thought that I could not feel any worse, I was to experience yet another aspect of war that I was not prepared to hear.

It happened while I was on another standard patrol with several other A.T.C.s about two months into my stint in Vietnam. I was talking to some other River Rats swapping stories when all of a sudden I seen him. I couldn't believe my eyes, but there he was. Alive! But how? There, plain as day, was Mazie.

I started to make my way up to him disbelieving more and more with each step I took. But something else was happening as well. The closer I got to him the more I noticed how empty he looked. The man I once knew was completely gone.

When I finally reached him I couldn't believe what I saw. I thought at first it was the injuries he had sustained from the shrapnel, but then I realized the change was in his eyes. We got to talking and after we did our typical reunion garbage he told me his story.

It seems the shrapnel had taken out one of his lungs, a kidney, and some of his ribs. The hospital thought for sure that he was a goner, so they prematurely sent his bride (they were married two weeks before he shipped out) a death notice. The all too familiar "we are sorry to inform you that your husband has died in the line of duty."

When he recovered from his injuries and was finally able to get a hold of her, she told him she couldn't deal with the uncertainty of war life. She just didn't want to deal with not knowing from day to day if he was alive or dead. It was just too much. With eyes full of tears, he said he couldn't blame her. She had asked him for a divorce and because he loved her so much, he couldn't refuse her.

After losing her he felt life just didn't mater anymore so although he could have gone home, he chose to stay in Vietnam. I told him that was crazy. All he had to do was go home and everything would have been fine. She wouldn't have to worry about weather or not he was alive because he would be there. He said he tried to tell her that but it was no use. Her mind had been made up and that was that.

I shook his hand and told him how sorry I was to hear about what happened. We spent the next hour just talking about what was going on back in the states, and laughing about memories from basics.

I walked away from my chance meeting with a guy that I had thought died; understanding that not all casualties of war happen in combat. With that in mind I headed back to my boat and wrote a letter to my beloved Phyllis. Grateful for such a wonderful person standing beside me.

CHAPTER 7

LETTERS FROM HOME

I wanted to tell Phyllis about everything that had happened since I last wrote her, but then thoughts of Mazie's wife kept coming into my mind. Would she be able to deal with everything going on over here? What would she think of me if I did tell her? It was hard enough for me to accept some of the things I had to do, let alone ask her to. For crying out loud we met at a Christian Bible camp, how could I tell her that I not only killed another human being, but that I killed a baby. I could barely accept what I had done, and I knew that I had no choice.

After sitting there staring at the blank paper in front of me for what seemed like hours, struggling with my thoughts, I decided that she could probably handle whatever I told her, but why would I give her more to worry about than she already had. Besides, I could always explain the other stuff to her when I was home.

With that in mind, I began my letter with how much I missed her and how I was glad that she would be there when I got back. I told her just bits and pieces of what had happened over the past few weeks so she could get the general idea of what was really going on without having her have to deal with the thought that the man she loved could commit such horrible sins. Talk about doing a tap dance number.

I told her about the guys on the boat and our luxurious bathroom facilities, as well as the way we pulled over the sampans for inspections. I wrote briefly about the quick V.C. attacks, but stressed how lousy they were at really hitting anything so as to tone down the reality of what it was really like.

To end the letter on a positive note, I told her about my one-week R&R coming up. I bragged that the Navy would pay for us to go to either Hawaii or Sidney, Australia, whichever one she preferred. As for myself, getting away from this hell would be vacation enough, but to see Phyllis again, especially in either dream location, would be like being in heaven.

I finished the letter with some final mushy sentiments, sealed it, then grabbed another sheet of paper and began a letter to my Mom and Dad.

Writing to them was a little easier then writing to Phyllis because I knew they had been through their own war time experiences, and would understand more about what I was going through, even if I didn't write it down. However, in the end, I still left out most of the gruesome details, because even though they would understand it, that didn't mean they needed to hear it.

I began with giving, an all be it limited version, of how I had lost all my gear 8 hours after I got there. Leaving out the part where the building fell on me, I wrote how the motor fire left me with only the clothes on my back which, because of the unbearable heat and humidity, I had decided to chop into shorts and a sleeveless shirt. After blasting the Navy's reluctant ability to replace anything, I told them about the black market.

Knowing that my parents would never approve of such things, I quickly explained that the clothes I was wearing were quickly rotting away, and that if I didn't do something soon, I wouldn't have anything to wear at all. I let them know that the process was very simple, held no risk to me, and would only cost me some of the sea rations that I wouldn't even eat if my life depended on it anyway.

As I sat there thinking of what else I should say, Maize's wife crept once again into my thoughts. I wondered again exactly how Phyllis was doing with me gone. As we were married not long before I left, I knew my parents didn't know her very well and although I knew they would have no problem checking on her if I asked, I didn't want to put either them or Phyllis in an awkward position.

In the end, I decided that she was now their daughter-in-law and that made her part of their family as well. Therefore, asking them to check on her suddenly seemed more natural somehow. Yet I still did not want to give them the wrong impression of her like she could not handle things for herself, so I decided to make my request seem like a "by the way if you get around to it" sort of thing.

I kind of figured she would be ok, but I didn't see the harm of them showing concern for their new daughter-in-law. If anything, it would make her feel more welcomed within the family if they showed her concern even when I was not there.

When I left she seemed to handle the idea of me being over there pretty well, but on the other hand, having your husband away at war so soon after being married could not be easy. I quickly dismissed all my negative thoughts away and went on to finish my letter.

I reassured them that I was ok and was looking forward to coming home as soon as I could. Home. I never realized what that word really meant until I got to Vietnam. Funny how something positive could come from something so horrible. It actually took being in a war zone to make me realize how much those closest to me really mattered. How sad is that.

As I sat there scolding myself for my lack of family involvement, I came to the realization that I couldn't do anything about the past, but the future, now that was another story. With that my thoughts came back to Bryn.

He was just about ready to graduate high school and was talking about joining the Marines soon after. I knew the choice was his, but having worked with a few Marines, I had come to know what that decision would entail and I just couldn't bare the thought of him going through all that.

It's funny. Before all this crap started I really didn't hang around my brothers too much. Ross was too young, and Bryn was busy with his then girlfriend, now wife, Colleen. In fact the only time we ever really did anything together away from the rest of the family was when I was dating Cathy, Colleen's sister, and we went on church outings together. But somehow the thought of my little brother getting caught up in all this was suddenly more then I could stand. Being the big brother I decided it was my "duty" to voice my opinion.

The problem was how do I get my point across about how rough things are over here, without causing my Parents any more worries. I decided that my parents would have to handle whatever extra pressure my concerns would bring. My main concern at that point was to keep my brother safe. I was over here. And according to Uncle Sam and me, that was enough sacrifice that any one family should have to endure. So consequences be damned, I told my Mom and Dad what a marines life was like over here, and that they should talk Bryn out of enlisting no matter what it took.

I once again told them how much I missed them and to try not to worry too much about me. I closed with a simple I love you all, your son Mark. Sealed the letter, grabbed the one I had written to Phyllis, and headed to the base post office to mail them.

As I was walking across the base, I found myself thinking how mail sure seemed a lot easier to get out then to get in. There is no lonelier feeling in the world then when mail call came and you had nothing to open. In fact I think I had been in country for more than a month before I received my first letter. When my mail did finally manage to find me, I was given a pile so large, I could barely grab it with one hand, ¾ of them from my Mom, and the rest from Phyllis.

I was in heaven. Just the sight of my mother's and wife's handwriting on the outside of the envelopes sent my heart soaring. I had not been forgotten.

The only way I can describe how much letters from home mean to a combat soldier is to have you think back to your earliest childhood Christmas memory with all those presents under the tree. And getting a package... that's like opening up the one gift you had been begging your parents for for weeks and they told you you couldn't have it, but yet there it was under the tree... that is only a fraction of how much letters from home mean to a combat soldier.

I was no different. I took my pile of gold and headed for my bunk and opened each letter savoring each word like a dog enjoys a beefed up bone.

My Mom wrote about various church doings and tidbits from my aunts and uncles. She would go on and on about Bryn and Ross and what they were up to and how Dad had to go collect rent over at their rental property. Each word making me more and more homesick but I couldn't stop reading.

My letters from Phyllis were filled with the typical mushy stuff as well as whatever she had going on in her life. She would write about some funny thing that happened at work, or something she read about in the paper. Each letter returning my heart to those warm nights at camp when we first met. Holding hands and first kisses. For a split second, I almost forgot where I was.

When I had managed to read through every letter, I picked them up and started reading them all over again. Picking up on the little sentiments between each line I had missed the first time through. It was then that two of my Mom's letters stood out more then the others.

The first one was a letter that casually mentioned a visit my father had made to Phyllis. It seems that he felt something "odd" was afoot, but that it was probably nothing, and even if it was, there was no sense of me worrying about anything until I came home anyway. Chalking it up to a misunderstanding, I concentrated more on the second letter that captured my attention. In that letter, my Mom explained a little campaign she had started.

It seems that my Mom took to heart that her son had to go so long without any clothes or gear, so she decided to write a carefully written letter to Wisconsin Senator William Proxmire. She explained what had happened to my gear, and that after a month I still had not received any replacements yet, and asked if the Senator could do anything about it.

Whenever I think back to this I find myself thinking about the movie "Tank", with Games Garner. The scene where Shirley Jones, goes to some political guy, and says that "I am either going out there and telling those people that you are a kind man who cares about the people or I'm going to tell them you're a complete asshole! What's it going to be!" Now I know my mother would never swear, but this is the image I get in my head every time.

I was highly impressed by her gumption, but I honestly thought she was wasting her time. I would soon find myself eating my words. Within two weeks of her letter, I not only had more clothes then when I started, but I had an extra pair of boots as well. Way to go Mom!

After that first bundle of gold came, mail call always had something for me. My Mom even managed to send me from time to time packages of canned ham, candies, newspaper clippings, anything she could think of to make her son's life a little better while he was away serving his country.

Now that I find myself looking back to that awful time, I truly believe it was those letters and packages from home that got me through. But not all the letters I got from home were as revitalizing as those first few months.

My Mom's letters continued to be full of details about Ross and his teenage adventures, Dad and his garden, work with the church and rental properties. But the ones that disturbed me the most, were the letters about Bryn, and the ones about, and from, Phyllis.

My Mom would tell me more and more with each letter about how firm Bryn was becoming about joining the Marines. He was bound and determined to "do his part" to prevent communism. If I were at home I would have beat him senseless.

I knew writing to him directly would be pointless, it might even push him towards the Marines even more. I just wish I could show him that the commercials he was seeing on TV were not showing the experiences he would be having if he were here in Vietnam. But how do you explain the realities of war to an impressionable teenager?

My only hope was that my tour of duty would end before he was able to enlist himself to an early grave.

As for Phyllis, well, I was getting some pretty unusual vibes from not only my Mom, but from the fewer and fewer letters I was getting from her as well.

When I first started getting mail, I would get quite a few letters from her. After about six months or so they became less and less frequent, and the letters she did send, seemed for the lack of a better word, cold.

It almost seemed like she was trying to justify something, but for the life of me I couldn't figure out what that something could possibly be. She would write about things that her father did to her when she was a child, and how that was effecting some of the decisions she was making now.

She would also write about how she felt that my parents were interfering in her life in some way, and that she wished they would just leave her alone instead of spying on her like she was doing something wrong.

I knew my Mom and Dad had been checking up on her per my request, but I never meant for her to feel like it was an intrusion. Yeah I know my Mom can be a bit much at times, but I thought my Dad's calm and nurturing persona would equal that out. How could I have been so wrong about this?

Phyllis seemed to be ok with my family before I left, what could have gone so wrong. Of coarse Phyllis was blaming my folks, but with each letter I got the impression that it wasn't my folks that were causing the problem. She would say things like if people would leave me alone I would be ok.

Her letters that were once sealed with love and kisses were now sponged with sarcasm and irritation. My only hope was that when we got together on my R&R I could get to the bottom of whatever was bugging her.

Speaking of my R&R Phyllis had managed to write that she would like to go Hawaii so I made all the required arrangements for us to meet there. I was so excited about seeing her again that the bad vibes I was getting from her letters seemed to disappear. I found myself counting the days before we would be together again.

But in the mean time I was just glad to have those magical uplifting tidbits from home. Especially the packages my Mom sent. Those were the best.

You see it became a tradition among my shipmates that whenever anyone would get a package from home we would all share its contents with each other. It kind of made you the hero of the day whenever you got an especially large one.

I remember once my Mom had sent me a rather large package of canned hams, candy, homemade cookies, and magazines, among other treats, and we all snacked on that package for a week. But getting packages from home had another advantage as well.

You see the more food you got from home, the less you had to rely on your sea rations. And although that was a reward in and of itself, we found that we could put those sea rations to a much better use.

It seems that the sea rations that we hated so much, were as good as cash when dealing with the Vietnamese Black Market. And they could get us things that you would never believe.

CHAPTER 8

THE BLACK MARKET
OF VIETNAM

The S.V. Black Market was by far the easiest way to get whatever you needed. It didn't matter what it was; the Black market always had it. From beer to Jack Daniels, to military supplies, the black market was the place to go.

But the best thing about purchasing anything from the black market was that the marketeers always accepted sea rations for whatever they had. And as far as we were concerned, they could have them. Isn't it funny how one mans trash is another mans gold.

From what I understood the black market was scattered throughout South Vietnam, but the only part of it that I got to know was the branch that worked off the Mekong delta. All one had to do was to flag down any sampan on the Delta, tell the occupants what you were looking for, negotiate how many sea rations it would take, then they would go off in search of your request.

Usually the sampan would return in about an hour or two with whatever you had asked for, you gave them the sea rations, it didn't matter which ones, and then you each went on your separate ways.

Some of the sampan operators were so good they would even shout across the Delta asking if anyone wanted various items. I was amazed at what these people could come up with. Believe it or not, in one of the hottest climates on earth, they could even supply us with ice. Yes Ice.

Not all things about the black market were good though. The Vietnamese people are very poor. So poor that they had to make indescribable choices. Choices that had they been anywhere else they might not have made. One of those choices was to sell a daughter; sometimes as young as 14 or even younger, to the Black Marketeers just so they could save the rest of their family.

Its easy to pass judgement on this but if you had to make the choice of selling a daughter into prostitution, or burring more of your family due to starvation, what would you do? The daughters being sold were guaranteed survival and it more often then not, guaranteed the future of the rest of the family.

Now granted women did not hold a lot of respect in the Vietnamese culture at that time, but still the choice to sell a member of ones family to ensure the survival of the rest, could never be an easy one, no matter what the circumstances.

Their keepers and the GIs treated the girls fairly well. The GIs all had the fear of being caught, which held with it very stiff consequences, and the Marketeers needed to protect their assets.

The girls themselves would get free food, booze and cigarettes, in exchange for sexual favors. More often then not, the girls that were sold stood a better chance of survival then those that stayed with their families. I'm not saying this was an ultimate life, but like I said difficult times, call for difficult choices.

The Marketeers would go up and down the Delta calling out "hey GI I got number one girl, you want boom boom?" The GI and the Marketeers would then haggle over how many sea rations or money the situation would require, then the Marketeer would have the girl escorted to the GI, then picked up at the prearranged time.

I personally didn't know anybody who took advantage of such occasions, but from what I understood through common knowledge, these girls were a pretty hot commodity at times.

My first exposure to the black market occurred within the first week I was in country. Some of my fellow shipmates that had been in country for a while had shown me how to bargain sea rations for whatever I would need.

However it wasn't until I was in country for over a month wearing the same shirt and cut off greens that I decided to finally give the black market a try. I decided to forgo the underwear, as it was so hot and humid I ditched them within the first two days anyway, and simply asked for two shirts and two pairs of greens.

I worked the deal, and an hour or two later the marketeer showed up with my new clothes. I fought the overwhelming temptation to strip right then and there and decided to wait until later that night to enjoy my new acquisition. After all I knew that we were heading back into base that night and a few hours more of wearing my now shredding garments wouldn't make much difference.

Once we docked for the night and secured our boat, I grabbed a new shirt cut a pair of the greens into shorts and headed across the base to the showers like a kid running to a carnival. I scrubbed my skin raw trying to get every last bit of grime off of me, got dressed, combed my hair, brushed my teeth, and strolled through the base a new man.

About a month or so later I decided to try my luck again and bargained for a blanket. That blanket was the softest warmest blanket I ever owned. If I could find one today I would buy it in a heartbeat. I was sorry almost instantly when I left it behind.

From that point on using the black market became somewhat of a monthly thing, more if someone on the crew needed something. In fact, it was not unusual for the crew of the boat I was on to pitch in together to get cases of Pepsi and beer, ice and even on occasion French bread.

Here we were in the middle of a war zone, in unbelievable heat, N.V.A. and V.C. shooting at us whenever they got the urge, yet we were still able to get cold Pepsi and beer. How cool was that.

Over my 13-month stay in Nam I managed to acquire besides whatever clothes I needed, a tape recorder, a Polaroid camera, as well as the occasional Pepsi from time to time.

You know it was funny, in the end I got more supplies from the black market then I ever did from the Navy.

So I'm sure by now you're asking yourself, if dealing with the black market was so great, why didn't you use them more often? Well, you see, we knew, or at least had a pretty good idea anyway, that the sea rations we were using as cash, were probably being given to the V.C. Which meant that we were actually, in a way, feeding those bastards that were trying to kill us every time we bought anything.

This kind of put a damper on things. But, when you are out in country for weeks at a time, with the temperatures in and above the 90's, and a humidity level well over 100%, a cold soda was more addictive than cocaine to an addict. And I challenge anyone who experienced the firefights we had to endure, not to want a shot of Jim Beam or Jack Daniels from time to time. I know I did and I was never a big drinker in the first place.

So yea, buying anything from the black market was probably not in our best interest, but as I have said, war forces you to make decisions that you would normally never make.

CHAPTER 9

WHY WE WERE CALLED RATS

One of Merriam Webster's Collegiate Dictionary definitions of a rat is "a contemptible person". I couldn't think of a better way to describe what we were. Sometimes we would go weeks without a shower; we learned how to scrounge for whatever we needed to survive, and we committed horrific acts of self-preservation, some to horrible to mention even today.

But I guess one of the biggest reasons we were called Rats, was that everyone hated to see us coming. It seams everyone knew we were just going to take whatever we wanted whether they liked it or not. Yes I guess you could say we built a bad reputation for ourselves, but we were also in a horrible situation.

The MRF (Mobile Riverine Force), otherwise known as the Brown Water Navy, was established in December of 1965 to help monitor the traffic on the Mekong Delta. The beauty of the MRF was that almost any military branch found a way to use our services.

We helped escort Seals and Marines into hot landing zones, then played babysitter to their boats while they went in and took care of business. Hell even the Army used us to transport their troops. All in all, I guess you can say we were the grunts behind the scenes, but that doesn't mean we didn't see our fair share of action.

But somehow, even though we were more often then not on the front lines of some pretty heavy artillery fire, we always seemed to be overlooked when it came to recognition. If a mission went well it was because the Seals did their job, or because the Army infantry kicked ass. What about the guys who themselves had to enter a firefight of their own, just to get the troops where they needed to be.

It was so frustrating to hear this unit talk about going back to a nice shower and hot food. Or even the steak and beer party the military was supplying them. The closest thing we got to hot food is when we took small amounts of c4 in a can, lit it, then put another can loosely on top of it, or if we had to go to the repair ship. And showers, we were lucky if we got to take one shower a week.

In a way we are still the forgotten ones today. Whenever you see any book written about Vietnam, there are pages and pages of the other military outfits, while you would be hard pressed to find even a paragraph written about us. Even then it is usually about the swift boats or the PBRs. It seems we men on the ATC's were insignificant in the scheme of things.

Now don't get me wrong. I have worked with just about every branch and unit type that was in Vietnam, and believe you me, they earned my respect hands down. I would never even think of taking anything away from them. And furthermore, I will defend the work they did till the day I die. It's just that we too put our lives on the line everyday, and although we were a group of scroungers, we still deserve to be recognized for what we accomplished.

Scroungers. Does that word fit us to a tee. You see being, an all be it temporary outfit, designed for just the Vietnam war, we didn't have a steady line of supplies. The guns we used were substandard rifles that became outdated for other units, and we never had enough ammunition for them. In fact this is one of the many reasons we had to go scrounging from other units. We simply could not do our jobs with what we were given.

It seems strange to say that you scrounged weapons from other ally units, but we knew if they lost their equipment they would have replacements within a day or two. For us we could never get the kind of equipment the other units had.

I must say that we weren't totally without scruples though. Whenever we would relieve a more up to date weapon from a parked jeep, we always left our substandard ones in their place. After all, we didn't want to leave the soldiers with anything to fight with should the need arise. If I had to choose though, I would say the men on the repair ships hated us the most.

You see, like I said, we were in country for sometimes three weeks at a time without taking a shower. You can imagine how we must have smelled after being out in that hot and humid climate without bathing. So when we got on those repair ships that were fully equipped with shower facilities, we took full advantage of them. More often then not, ignoring the customary time limit requested per shower.

We also helped ourselves, most gluttony, to their chow lines full of hot fresh food. Hey they got this kind of food everyday. We were lucky if we got that kind of luxury once every three months. You bet your ass we were going to take advantage of it. Hell some of them even had ice cream machines.

I can remember a time when I had come aboard an extremely modernized coast guard ship located as far away from the actual fighting that you could possibly be yet still be considered to be in a war zone. I had been sent by my captain to retrieve a bundle of mail for us guys on the front lines and was passing through the mess hall of the ship when I overheard the most asinine conversation I had ever heard.

There were a group of about 6 guys sitting at a clean table, each one had on a spotless uniform and had a plate full of hot food in front of them. They actually had the nerve to complain about the conditions they had to live under on this ship. Oh hell no!!!!!

It was more then I could stand, so I went up to the table and said: "You know you guys are sitting here with hot food, 3 meals a day, clean facilities with hot showers, movies and midnight snacks!" "You know where I sleep!? In a cot hanging from the rafters of an ATC!" "Every morning we have to sweep at least 7, 6 foot snakes off of our decks, and you guys are bitching about this!" "Why don't you come live in my shoes for a day, never knowing when the V.C. are going to attack!" "Then come back and complain about your lives here!" I walked away still tasting the bitter words that I had just spew at them, when I realized that not one of them said another word until I was long gone.

I got back on the PBR that escorted me to the ship, feeling that I had at least stood up for those of us those assholes looked down their nose at. There were many things I could understand about the reputations we had gotten, but to listen to those guys complain about their luxurious conditions, while they looked down on those of us on the lines, scrounging for scraps, was just more then I think anyone could take.

It was people like that, that also looked down on us for our willingness to openly use the Vietnamese Black Market. We knew they felt it was because of the black market that they could not get what they wanted when they wanted it. But for us, it was the only way we could get anything we needed.

For example, if I had waited for the Navy to replace my gear, the only set of clothes I had would have disintegrated to a point of being better off not wearing anything at all.

I guess in the end, I can understand why we were called rats. If I were on the outside looking in, I guess I would think the same thing. But, at least for me, I wear the title of "River Rat" with honor. I know what we did, and why we did them. And, had those people who looked down on us been in the same position we were in, I guarantee they would have probably done the same thing.

You see we did what we had to do. We were the bottom of the totem pole, and the last ones to get anything we needed. If we didn't do the scrounging we did, many of those troupes that depended on us doing our jobs, might not have made it.

Yeah we were scroungy. And yes we were gluttons when we got to anyplace that had hot food. But all in all, us "River Rats" saved the lives of many troops during our stay in Vietnam. That to me justifies anything else we had to do.

CHAPTER 10

COMBING FORCES

One of our primary jobs in Vietnam, was to supply aid and support, wherever and whenever, we were needed. During my tour in Nam, I can remember working with just about every branch of service that was over there. Marines, Army, Navy Seals, Mercenaries, and even some sharpshooters from time to time. But the worst for me was when we were asked to pick up S.V. locals.

You see these are very poor people, and they learned, rather quickly, that U.S. GIs like to have comfortable surroundings. Things like cameras, radios, tape recorders, and lots of sea rations. And they knew that the black market would pay them for everything they could get their hands on. So whenever they would come on board a U.S. boat, they would scrounge around taking anything they could get their hands on.

Thing was, that we had to maintain our posts on the boat at all times, because the V.C. could attack at any time. Leaving our post could mean the difference between life and death, so even when we knew these people would probably rob us blind, there wasn't much we could do about.

However, there was a time when I left my post on the pretense of "getting some more ammo." I went below deck to where we had the ammo stored, and I found a S.V. going through some of the crew's things. He whipped around and showed me his handgun, but I showed him that I already had my pistol out and pointed right at him.

He looked at me like I had my nerve confronting him, but he dropped the stuff he had swiped on the floor, and went back up top. I was thinking to myself, "gee sorry to disappoint you bud."

It was things like that, that caused us Rats to despise these people. In fact, we had such a hatred for them, that their welfare became less and less significant to us. I was no different. However, I didn't realize how numb my feelings for these people were, until one day they were put to the ultimate test.

It started out as a routine morning for us until the captain of our boat informed us that we had been given orders to pick up 35 or so S.V. locals and escort them a mile or two up the Delta back to their village. We all mumbled to ourselves "great, better go lock up everything."

We picked them up and they scattered around the boat like normal. But when one of the guys from the crew noticed one of them making his way below deck, he cut him off and showed him his pistol. The S.V. put his head down and hi-tailed it back to the flight deck with some of the others.

About three miles or so up river, we came to a trail barley visible in the thick jungle. The captain pulled up to the shoreline and they all got out disappearing through the over grown brush.

After the last person made his way into the jungle, the captain pulled away from the shore and I made my way back to the opposite side of the ship to enter my gun mount for our return trip up the Delta.

I got about ½ way across the boat when I heard the most gut wrenching scream I had heard since the B.G. shot the second prisoner off the bow of our boat.

I turned around just in time to see one of the younger men that we had just dropped off encircled by something very large, shinny, and sleek in nature. A split second later, the man was gone.

The next thing I knew, the villagers were all lined up along the shoreline throwing percussion grenades into the murky water. I sat watching as they threw their barrage of more then 20 grenades, any one of which should have killed anything in the water for no less then 60 –70 yards, yet nothing came back up.

There should have been body pieces of both the villager and whatever the thing was that grabbed him, but nothing. To me, it meant that whatever grabbed him was either awful quick, really really big or both.

By this time the rest of the crew had come to the side of the boat to see what all the commotion was about. I explained to them what I had seen to which the captain only said two words before walking away; ocean snake. Seeing how we were only 3 clicks, from the ocean I believed him.

If it was at all possible, I guess I had become somewhat accustomed to performing our daily "pest control" of the 6-7 visitors we had each morning. But the 5-6 foot snakes that caused us such aggravation on top of the boat, was nothing compared to the ones underneath it.

It was that day that I realized how much disdain I had for the S.V., because I could feel absolutely no remorse for the guy taken down by the snake. Instead my thoughts reverted to one of the units that I had come to respect the most. The Navy Seals.

The Navy Seals were the top notch of the service men in Vietnam. They knew what they were doing, and were used whenever all other units failed to reach their objectives.

Whenever we would assist them, it was certain to be a very active night. Typically, we would follow them into whatever hot zone they were headed to. When we would get to the intended location, the Seals would gather their gear, fire each gun once to check for accuracy, then would high tail it into the jungle to take care of whatever trouble they came to address.

Sometimes they would be sent in to set up an ambush. In these cases, we would just drop them off in the V.C. area at night, and would come back first thing in the morning. Funny thing was, by the time we had gotten there, they were always waiting for us. Usually with a few dead V.C. lying at their feet.

The one thing that I did notice, more than anything else, was they had some pretty strong weaponry. Where we had 20 mm, they had a 107 high explosive round on the front of their boat. And their handguns made ours look like cap guns. But then again, with what they had to face when they went into a hot zone, I could see why they needed better equipment that we did.

Two other groups that were known for their fighting skills, were the Marines and Army units. They too had far superior weaponry than we had, which by now I had come to the conclusion that everybody had better equipment than we had, for probably good reasons.

The army primarily used us for transporting troops, about 35-40 guys per ship.

We would drop them off at whatever hot location they were headed to, then we would head back to our base camp and continue on with our normal patrols.

They would go, in take care of business, then call us for a pick up, usually in about 2-3 days. But the coolest thing about hauling the Army troupes, was that they always left behind 20-30 full clips, and even the occasional gun to go with them. And, living up to our reputations of Rats, we were more than happy to take them off their hands. Sometimes I would even wonder if they were left behind as payment for getting them in and out of hot areas safely.

Heck we even supplied them with additional firepower from our boats when they were coming out of a hot zone that was still unsettled. We were very good at chasing off whatever it was that was coming after them. Usually that was because we had the grenade launcher and more powerful guns on our boats than the typical ground patrol would carry around with them.

The Marines also used us for troop transports, but also for something more sophisticated as well. Sometimes, going into a reported hot zone full bare was not always the best way to handle a situation. The Marines had a better tool at their disposal for handling random V.C. that would spread out along the shoreline of the Mekong Delta: Sharp shooters.

As a kid I would watch all those war movies that would show sharp shooters pointing a riffle at some target some ungodly distance away, than whatever they were aiming at explodes into smithereens. Well, I guess that plays for good drama, but the actual version of what a sharp shooter really does is much more, and sometimes less, impressive.

Generally, we would get the call that we were to escort a sharp shooter up and down part of the Delta that was experiencing more than average V.C. activity. Hell, usually it was us that put the call in.

Anyway, the sharp shooter would lay down on the flight deck behind 1-2 sand bags, and position his rifle with a front tripod for stability and a laser scope for better accuracy, comfortably in front of him. He would then place a radio on one of the sandbags anchoring it so it could be easily accessed, but wouldn't fall on the deck giving away his location on the boat.

When he gave the signal that he was ready, our captain would glide our boat as silently as possible down the infected section of the Delta. Usually these details happened at night, which made the laser scope so important. The sharp shooter would be able to detect the smallest movement in the jungle, take one shot, and then announce on the radio one kill. Continuing this, sometimes for hours, without taking his eye off the bank. Always counting the kills as he went along. It was that simple. Yet it was also, that impressive.

As much as we helped the other units, they too helped us when we found ourselves in situations beyond our capabilities. Mostly we called for air support. Those guys were damn good.

If we found that we were in need of "assistance" the air support would come in and drop their loads right on top of the N.V.A units. The next thing we knew the sky was lit with a beautiful black and orange glow, and the incoming shelling came to an abrupt stop.

We got to know the other units stationed in our area, if not by name than at least by reputation. Hell, we even learned a few games to play with each other that helped create a sort of bond between the units.

The Rats were no exception. We had started this thing with the chopper pilots where we would stand on our flight decks and hold a broom up over our heads. The pilot of the chopper would then come in and knock the broom out of our hand. Now that was impressive.

CHAPTER 11

R&R WITH PHYLLIS

I had been told shortly after I had gotten in country that everybody was given a weeks R&R sometime during their tour in Nam. Mine came almost exactly 6 months after I got there. I was given the option of either Hawaii or Australia, but even better was that the Navy would pay for Phyllis to join me at either location.

After Phyllis wrote to me that she preferred Hawaii, I made all the arrangements and after a lot of red tape, I finally managed to secure all our plans. I was to board a commercial flight out of Saigon, and Phyllis was scheduled to leave out of Milwaukee so that our flights would land at as close to the same time as possible.

I couldn't believe it. I was actually on my way to see Phyllis. It would be the honeymoon that we never got. Just the thought of seeing her again sent my heart soaring higher then the plane that was bringing me to her.

When the plane finally landed, I grabbed my bag and headed for the place where we prearranged to meet with wings on my feet. There, I found her there waiting for me. Her shoulder length red hair flowing in the breeze, looking just as pretty as the day I met her. We ran to each other and held each other close, neither one wanting to let go. Suddenly everything that happened over the past 6 months was all a blur. We were back together again, and for now, that's all that mattered.

We released each other long enough to grab our bags then walked through the airport arm in arm to the nearest car rental place. Then after crossing the T's and dotting the I's, we got into our rental car and headed off for our week of paradise.

I had arranged for us to stay, free of charge, at the Pearl Harbor naval base on the big Island of Hawaii. I knew that I was taking a big chance staying on the base, but as far as I was concerned, all we needed was a clean bed, and a hot shower, and we would be as happy as two people could be. But still, I wasn't quite sure what we were in for.

As it turns out, we were put up in this one room shack that had a dresser a bath and a somewhat clean bed. But at that point, we just didn't care. We threw our bags on the floor then let our passion consume us. We spent that first night holding each other close, each afraid that it was all a dream and we would wake up half the world apart again.

We talked well into the night until we just couldn't fight sleep anymore. Trained to not give in to sleep, I watched as she closed her eyes and drifted off into a peaceful slumber, stroking her hair and kissing her face as gently as I could careful not to wake her. I don't know how long I laid there, all I know is that lying next to her gave me the first peaceful nights sleep I had gotten since I went away to basics.

We woke the next morning refreshed and ready to start our week in paradise. I only had one complaint. I was not going to spend our week in paradise dawning the same dreary military garb I was forced to wear in Nam, so we set out to buy the brightest Hawaiian outfits we could find.

We hopped in our rental car, rushed off the base, and pulled into the first store we came to. I ended up buying an obnoxiously blue shirt with huge white flowers and a pair of readymade shorts. Phyllis matching dress not only amply displayed her voluptuous suntanned figure, but managed to enhance the color of her sexy red hair as well.

Having the wardrobe situation under control, we decided to set out for some breakfast. I can't tell you how great that first taste of real eggs, bacon, potatoes, and coffee was. In fact, I was so glad to have real food in front of me, that I didn't think to ask her why she wasn't eating.

After breakfast, we decided to take a drive around the big island. Even with the couple of stops we made to get a better look at a particularly amazing sight, the whole trip only took about 45 minutes. But the whole time I kept sneaking peaks over at Phyllis, feeling like I must have been the luckiest man on earth to have such a great wife. She was all I could ever ask for in a woman, and more.

Phyllis spent most of the ride staring out the window, I assumed admiring the scenery that somehow managed to become more beautiful after each turn. She seemed unusually quiet, but I chalked that up to the long day we each had the day before. Between the long flight from Milwaukee, and the active night we had, it seemed only natural that she would be a little out of sorts.

But still, she seemed a little put out whenever I would ask her if she was ok, passing off her distance as her just being tired or that I was just imagining things.

Knowing that we only had a week together, I didn't want to unnecessarily upset her. So I took her hand and suggested that we head back to the base, and get some rest before dinner, which she readily agreed to.

After we had slept for a couple of hours she seemed to be back to her old self again, so I asked her if she was up to going to a Luau that was being held a short distance from the base. She said that a luau sounded like fun and proceeded to get ready to head out.

That night we had a great time watching the after dinner show together. The various performers were absolutely fantastic, and we found ourselves being swept up in all the activity surrounding us. We laughed until our sides hurt, forgetting all about the unpleasantries of earlier. She really seemed to be back to her old self again.

After the luau, we again headed back to the base for another night of peaceful slumber. Although I detected her fading back into her own world again, I decided not to press her about it for the rest of our trip.

Our third day on the Island we decided to go to sea world. And although Phyllis bounced back and forth between having a good time and slipping back into her thoughts, I would say the day was pretty good.

The rest of the week we spent just touring the island, shopping this store and that, doing your typical tourist crap. All the while I kept getting the feeling that Phyllis wanted to tell me something.

I would catch her staring at me with a far away look in her eyes like she had a deep dark secret eating away at her, but she just couldn't bring herself to say the words that were tearing her up inside.

Then alas it came, our last night on the island. We spent much of that night walking hand in hand along the beach, talking about whatever came to our minds. Everything that is except what was really on her mind.

When we got back to the base for our last night together, we each packed up our bags then crawled back into bed for the last time until I came home for good. I went to pull her close but she protested that she needed to get some sleep before her long flight home again. She rolled her back to me and we fell asleep side by side but somehow further apart then when I was in Nam.

The morning we were scheduled to leave, I dreaded putting back on those putrid military issue clothes. I took one last look at my colorful Hawaiian shirt before tossing it into my bag, threw the last of my things on top of it then closed it up, and put it in the trunk of our rental car. When Phyllis had finally finished packing up all her things, I put her bags in the trunk as well, and we began our final moments together in paradise.

As I drove the short distance to the airport, we talked a little about the various things we had done over the week, making any small talk we could think of so we could avoid talking about what we both knew we really needed too.

As I returned the keys to our rental car, Phyllis grabbed our bags out of the trunk, looking almost relieved that the week was over. I pacified myself into thinking that I was reading way to much into her behavior, and that it was probably just the result of going home alone while I went off once again to face an uncertain fate.

We each grabbed our individual bags, gave each other a quick kiss goodbye, then each headed off to our separate flights. Her's heading back to a warm bed, home cooked meals, and hot and cold running water. Mine bringing me to a war that showed no mercy to either side.

CHAPTER 12

CHANGING BOATS

Shortly after I got back form Hawaii, the powers that be decided to turn over the defense of South Vietnam to its people. This was very significant because it meant, for the Americans anyway; there was a light at the end of the tunnel. But it also meant that we had to revert back to the original concept of training the South Vietnamese to defend their own land.

For the River Rats, it meant that a few of us would be transferred onto other boats so the S.V. could learn how to run the boats that have been so crucial in the effort to stop the N.V. supply lines. I happened to be one of the guys to be transferred.

At first I was a little miffed leaving the crew I had come to know so well that we could practically read each other's minds; a skill that came in handy during the many firefights that we found ourselves in. We each knew our jobs, and we had come to trust each other with our lives. More than that, I had come to think of these guys as family. But alas, when you're the grunt, you go where you're told to go. So with a heavy heart, I went below deck and started gathering my things.

As I got below deck, I started looking around at my floating cot, and my own personal space for my collected luxuries. I started thinking about having to spend the rest of my tour sleeping in the hot and musty hull of a boat when another thought crossed my mind. How was I going to pack all my crap into my duffel? After three tries and practically bursting out the sides, I managed to fit everything in.

Now for the hard part; saying goodbye to the guys. Not wanting to get too mushy, I simply shook hands with everyone on board, then headed out to my new station.

When I got my first glimpse of the boat, the first thing I noticed was that I had gone from a hard top A.T.C. to a ragtop. The boats are primarily the same, except that the hard top allowed for a chopper pad on its bow, which I had used for listening to my radio on quiet night.

The second thing I noticed was on the back of the boat, in between the gun mounts, someone had painted the words "The Fickle Finger of Fate." As most people who grew up in that era can tell you, those words became quite famous with regards to the Vietnam War.

After giving the words a quick chuckle, I boarded the boat and said some quick greetings to my new shipmates. One of the guys came up and showed me around the boat and where I could store my gear. When he pointed to a bunk mixed in with others on the floor of the hull I just looked up and said what about there. I pointed up to the rafters and the guy laughed and said, "sure buddy what ever." He walked away laughing and went up top again.

I asked the captain if we were shipping out anytime soon, and he said not until the next day. I then asked if I could go into the base for something and he shrugged his shoulders and said "why not."

When I came back to the boat carrying a medical stretcher and some rope, the crew just looked at me for a minute and then went on with whatever they were doing. I spent the next hour or so duplicating my previous sleeping arrangements and storing my gear, when the captain came down, looked at what I had done, shook his head giving me a crooked smile and said "not bad, Purdy is it".

After I had gotten settled in, I decided I had better get to know the people that I would assumedly spend the rest of my tour with. There were 4 Americans and 2 S.V.s that I presumed were there for the same reason I was being transferred.

With all that I had experienced, and all that I heard of their reputations, I was a little apprehensive sleeping that night with 2 S.V. on board, but soon managed to drift off to a guarded rest.

The next day we were given the routine sampan patrol so we could continue the training of the S.V. I must admit that the one learning how to drive the boat did ok, although I was much more comfortable with the original driver at the helm, but the second S.V. in charge of engine repair was, to be polite, useless. He was always complaining about how hot the engine area was, or that he was tired and needed to lie down.

I was to find out later that this was a typical complaint among all the A.T.C. S.V. trainees. Talk about frustrating. Here we were, in their country, fighting their war for them, and they were complaining about the conditions. What kind of bullshit was that? After I had listened to that crap for a couple of days, I had come to the conclusion that all this training was pointless. The minute we pulled out, the S.V. would take any boats we left behind, and use them for their homes, and the weapons would be sold to the black market for whatever they could get.

In the end, we all knew what was going to happen but we also knew that we were not going to pull out of Vietnam until the powers that be felt the S.V. were amply trained to defend themselves. So despite our reservations, we did what the powers that be told us to do.

The S.V. were not the only changes I had to get used to on the F.F.F. (Fickle Finger of Fate). After I had been with this crew for two weeks or so, I noticed one of the crew liked his marijuana a bit too much for my comfort. I understood the need to calm down in such a high-tension atmosphere, but when you have other peoples' lives counting on you, you owe it to them to be at your very best.

I decided after going through a rather intense battle with some V.C., that I was not about to die because this guy had a habit. Although I didn't know how the rest of the crew felt, I made up my mind that I had to at least talk to this guy. So one night I found myself sitting alone with him, so I decided to take a chance and tell him how I felt. Not wanting to piss him off, I simply told him "hey, what you do on your own time is up to you, but when were on patrol, what you do affects the rest of us as well."

At first I thought he was going to lose it on me, but then his war eyes turned suddenly soft, and I knew that he understood that what I said was right. He turned his eyes away from me and said something I knew came from his heart. He said, "I know I have a problem Purdy, but I would never let any member of this crew down, including you." He then got up and went back to his bunk and went to sleep.

I felt a little guilty about questioning him, but in the end it brought a new understanding between the two of us. He did keep his promise to me, and the rest of the crew though. He never once let us down when we were on patrol. And that's all I ever asked of him.

CHAPTER 13

MY FINAL DAYS IN VIETNAM

Generally speaking, every combat soldier keeps track of how much time they have left on their tour of duty. I was no different. I had been in country for just about a year, which meant that I only had one month left in that God forsaken hell hole, when I finally got my first break since I got to Vietnam.

It was a typical day in country, so we were getting our boat ready for the day's activities, when the captain of the boat gave me the news. I was being shipped out to a base camp in Dong Tam. I couldn't believe it. You mean, I was actually going to a place where I wouldn't be shot at every day. A place where there was food that wasn't heated by an explosive! A place where I could take a shower everyday! Yeah!!!!

My orders said that I was to be an American Advisor to the S.V. Which is a fancy title given to someone who simply teaches S.V. troops how to fill out the necessary forms to get their boat fixed. But hell, if it gets me off that damn boat, give me a pen.

When I started to pack, I decided that I wouldn't need some of things that I had acquired over the past year. I knew that clothing was hard to come by, legally anyway, while you were in country, so I left behind all but one outfit for the next guy. I also left behind my hanging sanctuary, hoping that someone else would find it as convenient as I did.

I also left behind my radio, whatever sea rations I had left, the blanket I had acquired from the black market (a move I would later come to regret), and whatever food I had left from various packages from home. I had put the rest in my ditty bag, and headed up top to say my final farewells to my shipmates.

I didn't think that saying goodbye would be so hard, yet when I think about it, maybe I should have. I mean these men and I have depended on each other for everything, including our mere survival. We had formed a bond that would last a lifetime, whether or not we would ever see each other again. Even today, the men on "the Fickle Finger of Fate," as well as those on the first boat I was assigned too, are forever engraved in my heart and thoughts.

After I had said my final good-byes, I took one last look around, then headed off to my new assignment.

I was to be stationed at a split Naval/Army base, which also housed some American civilians that were responsible for some kind of government funded construction work. I would come to find out, that these civilian groups were up for hiring ex military men for managerial purposes. Turns out, the pay was pretty good as well, but there was no way in hell, I was going to be in Vietnam, one second longer than I absolutely had to be. So I decided to stick with my current situation for as long as I had to, grateful for such luxuries as cold showers and powdered eggs.

After I had gotten settled in, I met with a lieutenant that laid down exactly what my job for the next month would be. He explained that since the U.S. government was starting to turn responsibility for defending South Vietnam over to its people, that we needed to train them on how to not only operate the machinery, but how to schedule maintenance on it as well. That's what my job was going to be.

I was told that I was to show pre-selected S.V. locals, what forms to fill out for which repairs. Then, how to explain to whoever their contact would be, what exactly they needed. Whether the repair required parts or just simple hands on maintenance, there were forms that had to be filled out so the mechanic knew what exactly had to be done.

For example, let's say a boat needed a simple oil change. The correct forms needed to be filled out explaining exactly what work would be required, then the S.V. would have to communicate with the mechanics as to what work they needed to have done. This sounds simple enough, but most of the S.V. could not read, or write English, which made getting repairs done down right impossible. My job was to teach them these skills.

Basically, my day began with a quick shower, then a leisurely hot breakfast at the mess hall, then off to my personal jeep. I would make sure I had plenty of gas to get wherever my destination was for the day, then it was off to my rounds.

After parking at the nearby base, I strolled down to the area where the boats were docked and asked if everything was ok. If I got the impression that my questions were not being understood, I would actually have to board the boat and use the universal language of shaking my head yes or no while pointing to various points on the boat that were known to require attention from time to time. Hey, it worked.

If they told me, or I found out by sheer luck, that a boat needed some maintenance done, I would either show the boat crew how to fill out the necessary forms, or fill them out myself. I would then file the forms with the maintenance crews, who would in turn schedule the required repairs. Yea, it was a tough job, but someone had to do it.

After a month of pointing and filing I was finally given what I waited 13 months for. I was given my orders to go home. I couldn't believe it. I made it. I was going home. I went to find a guy that I had met during those last few weeks, and told him about my orders, when he showed me his.

As luck would have it, we were scheduled to leave hell on the same plane, so we left the base together and headed for the airport. And get this; we were actually being flown home commercially. No more flying box, no more sitting on the floor for hours, and no more jumping out of moving airplanes.

When we got to the airport, we were mixed in with 70 other GIs all going home. We were told to dump out our duffel bags so they could be searched for illegal souvenirs, weapons, and other various items we would have no desire to bring home with us. Then it was onto the most beautiful sight I had ever seen. The plane that was bringing us home.

We felt like we were being flown first class, because the flight attendants treated us like celebrities. Together, the 70 GIs on board, drank the plane dry, and ate like kings. We hooted and hollered seemingly unable to contain our excitement over what we actually survived. That was the best flight I have ever taken.

When we reached California, we thanked the flight attendants for their kindness and understanding, and proceeded down the steps that lead us once again to American soil. With tears in his eyes, my friend got down on his hands and knees and kissed the ground; a tradition that had become increasingly popular with returning Vietnam Veterans.

Personally, I did something else to celebrate my homecoming. I dumped the contents of my duffel bag out onto the ground. I put aside my medals, my sieves, and my River Rat hat, then took everything else and dumped it in the nearest trashcan I could find.

We walked together until we reached the entrance of the airport, which would force us our separate ways. We shook hands, and said our farewells, then we each headed to our perspective flights that would send us home.

As I got onto the plane that would finish my 13 month long trip in hell, I couldn't help but reflect on what I had actually done. I not only survived a war zone, but I came back with absolutely no injuries.

Obviously, my parents and my prayers were answered. As I took my seat, and buckled my belt, I said a very long prayer, thanking God for watching out for me, and asked his forgiveness for the sins I had to commit while I was over there.

When the plane landed in Milwaukee, WI. I grabbed my bag and headed down to the baggage claim area, where my wife and a male friend of hers had come to pick me up. I gave her a kiss, dumped my bag into the trunk. Her friend was driving, and while I was putting my bag in the trunk, Phyllis slipped into the front seat next to him. As there was not enough room in the front seat for all of us, I decided to climb into the back seat, and we all headed down hwy I94 where I anxiously awaited to resume my life as an American civilian.

CHAPTER 14

LIFE AFTER VIETNAM

As we headed down the highway, I looked around at the scene unfolding around me, and for the first time, I realized how beautiful the city of Milwaukee really is. With its artfull construction of highways, that strategically overlook the shores of Lake Michigan and the lake itself that shown bright with the sun gleaming of its blue waters.

I found myself staring out over the water, at the many sailboats and pleasure crafts enjoying a peaceful day on one of the greatest lakes God ever made. I was so lost in my thoughts, that I didn't even realize we had turned off a different road than the one that should have brought us home.

When I finally did realized that we were indeed going down the wrong street, I asked Phyllis what was going on. She turned around and nonchalantly said that she didn't feel comfortable living in the same house as my parents anymore, so she decided to move across town.

Ok….. And the reason she wouldn't tell me this before was because…… Oh well, I guess it really didn't matter where we were living, as long as we were together.

Phyllis's friend dropped us off in front of a house in a rather rough area of Milwaukee. I was a little taken aback at the neighborhood, but at least the house was surprisingly large. In fact, I was wondering how she could manage such a large place, even in that neighborhood. My answer came rather quickly.

Phyllis led me up a flight of steps, which lead to a dingy attic, which had been converted into a small one-bedroom apartment. I couldn't believe what I was looking at. Why would she give up the place we had, for this! Granted, it wasn't the Ritz, but this place made it look like a palace.

I was lost for words, but I didn't want my first night home to begin with a battle, so I just kept my thoughts to myself. Phyllis showed me where I could store my things, and then told me that my parents wanted us to stop by. I was looking forward to thanking my mom in person for all the things she had done for me while I was in Nam, so I quickly cleaned up a little and we headed over to their place.

She had sent me so many packages and well written letters, that I felt her love surpassing all those miles, and whatever the N.V. could throw at me. But the best thing she had done by far, was waiting for me when we pulled up in front of their house.

It seems she had taken a white bed sheet, wrote the words "**WELCOME HOME MARK**" on it, then hung it from the roof so it covered the front of the house. It was the first time in 14 months that I truly felt like I was home. All I could do was stand there and cry when I saw that sheet flying in the wind. But more importantly, I felt more loved than I ever had.

I just stood on the sidewalk, letting the tears flow down, when my family came bursting through the front door. I grabbed my mom and hugged her for all I was worth. Next I turned to my dad and then to my brothers. After we all had a chance to hug and cry, we headed into the house where the table was set full of home cooking. Mom must have been cooking from the minute she found out I was coming home. She had made all my favorite foods. I cried again, and sat down on the couch, thinking how good it was to be home.

We spent most of the night catching up on all that I had missed while I was gone, and then the whole thing caught up to me. The liquor on the long flight back from Nam, the subsequent flight from San Francisco to Milwaukee, then all this emotional reunion. It was more then I could take. I told everybody that I appreciated everything they had done, but that I really needed to get some sleep. They all understood, gave me another hug, and it was home to Phyllis's house to restart our lives together.

I heard about how returning Veterans would have flashbacks for a while after they got back, but I never thought for a minute that it would happen to me. I was wrong. That first night I dreamt that I was back in Nam in the middle of a firefight. I woke up to Phyllis shaking me awake, telling me I was shouting in my sleep. I bolted straight up trying to regain my bearings, apologized to Phyllis for waking her up, then rolled over and laid there, afraid to go back to sleep.

The next morning when I had woke up; I found a note from Phyllis saying that she had to go to work. I made myself some breakfast, then took a long hot shower allowing the clean, hot as I could stand it water, just soak through my skin, until the water started running cold.

I got myself dressed and wandered around our little shack trying to figure out exactly what she saw in that place, when the phone rang. When I answered it, the man on the other end asked first who I was, then where Phyllis was. When I explained that I was Phyllis's husband, the guy hung up on me.

I decided to ask Phyllis about it later, but in the mean time I had to do something about where we were living. I headed to the bank and asked about a GI loan for a house and found that I qualified for a substantial amount.

Forgetting about the earlier phone call, I told Phyllis about the loan. She called in sick the next day and we went house hunting. We ended up finding a rooming house that we could afford, and started proceedings for purchasing the house.

A week later, we fond ourselves moving into a duplex that had 7-bedrooms upstairs that we turned into a rooming house for men, while Phyllis and I had the 3-bedroom apartment downstairs. I thought my prayers had been answered. Little did I know, that fate had some more surprises in store for me.

I had spent all my time renovating, the house and working again for my Uncle Kay. Then one day, I was looking for something in a drawer in our bedroom, when I found them.

It seems that my "wife" had been having sexual relations with not only one, but with quite a few of our male tenants, and I happened upon some half finished letters that she had been writing to some of the guys. Suddenly, it all made sense. Hawaii, moving away from my mom and dad, the guy that drove her to pick me up, the phone call the day after I got back, all of it. I sat on the bed shaking from anger.

When she got home from work that night, I confronted her with what I had found. She didn't even try to deny it. After calling her a few choice words, I told her that the house was mine, and that she had to leave that night. She packed a bag, and headed out the door. The next day, I contacted a lawyer, and filed for divorce.

My lawyer informed me that I had a clear-cut case of adultery, and should have no problem keeping the house because it was purchased with a GI loan. But Phyllis had one more trick up her sleeve. She was pregnant.

I couldn't take it any more. I decided to go to the one person I could always count on for love and support, my mom. She poured me a cup of coffee then sat down to listen to my troubles. When I went to pick up the cup, I found my hands were shaking so bad, that the only way I could drink the coffee she had poured, was to leave the cup on the table, and bend down and sip it from there.

I told her everything that had been going on since I got back, from the flashbacks, to Phyllis's adultery, and now the baby? I told her that sometimes I regretted even coming home from Vietnam, because at least there you knew who your enemies were.

Phyllis was claiming that the child was mine, presumably conceived in Hawaii, and consequently served me with an order to pay child support. Thinking that the child really was mine, I told myself that no matter what my feelings for Phyllis were, I was going to be a good father to my child. With that in mind, I had no problem paying the child support payments after the baby was born.

Phyllis gave birth to a baby boy shortly before our divorce was to be finalized, and I could not be happier to be a father, even if that meant I had to deal with Phyllis for the rest of my life. My son was worth it.

Around this time, I had met a young lady named Faya. She quickly became a friend that I could confide all my troubles too, but only a friend. She sympathized with the troubles I was having with Phyllis, and gave me some advise that would drastically turn things around for me, thus leaving me forever in her debt.

I told Faya about the baby being born way too early to be conceived in Hawaii, which caused me to have serious doubts to whether or not the child really was mine. She recommended that I demand a paternity test be taken. I asked my lawyer about it, and he set to arranging the test immediately.

Phyllis was furious. She tried every trick in the book to prevent the test from being taken, bringing more suspicion on her with every protest. Finally, she was forced by the courts to have the tests done on not only the baby, but her as well.

When the tests came back that the baby didn't have either my blood type, or hers, it was determined the child could in no way shape or form be mine. When my lawyer called me with the news, he told me I could stop paying child support payments if I wanted to. I hung up with him, and immediately called Faya with the news.

About two months later Phyllis and I were scheduled back in court to finalize our divorce. The judge swore us in, and reviewed the case in front of him, before asking my lawyer about the case. My lawyer explained about how the house was paid for by my GI loan, and then about the letters proving Phyllis's affair.

Phyllis lawyer was enraged. He asked to see the letters, which he was promptly given. He read just a few lines of the first letter written in Phyllis's handwriting, took one look at her, yelled at her for lying to him, then stormed out of the courtroom. But that was nothing compared to what the Judge did to her.

He proclaimed, that due to her infidelity, not only was my petition for a divorce granted, but that I was no longer required to pay child support or alimony. Phyllis's face was redder then her hair. I was ecstatic. I couldn't wait to call Faya and tell her what her suggestion regarding the paternity test had resulted in.

Shortly after my divorce was final, Faya and I became closer and closer and soon decided to start dating. We were very happy and started talking about making our relationship more permanent when Phyllis came up with another scheme.

It had been two months after our divorce was finalized, when I got a summons to appear, once again, in family court regarding failure to pay child support. I was pissed off. I called my lawyer and told him about the summons, and he just laughed. He asked if I still had my divorce papers. I reassured him that I had, so he said all I had to do was show up at court. I wasn't even going to need him, but that if by chance something were to go wrong, that he would take care of it.

Trusting his judgment, I did as he suggested, and went to court unrepresented. I was surprised when I wasn't even nervous when Phyllis's new lawyer started rambling on about my not paying child support. He explained that I owed Phyllis x amount of money in back child support payments, and then went on and on about some legal mumbo jumbo.

When he finished his spiel, the court commissioner trying the case asked me what I had to say. Having been very quietly listening to everything that her lawyer had been saying, I was glad to finally have the chance to set the situation straight once and for all.

I told the commissioner that I really didn't have anything to say, but that I did have something to show him. I gave him a folder containing my divorce papers, which explained that the reason I didn't have to pay child support, was because the child was the result of an affair Phyllis had while I was in Vietnam serving my country.

The commissioner angrily closed the folder I handed him, politely gave it back to me, and apologized to me for wasting my time. He then turned to Phyllis and his tone instantly turned.

He chastised her for wasting not only my time, but the courts and his time as well. He then turned on her lawyer saying that he should never have allowed this case to get to that point and he had better never let that happen again.

Her lawyer apologized to the court commissioner and said that he had no knowledge the issue had already been settled, then turned to Phyllis and said "you will be getting my bill for this!!!"

I left that courtroom knowing that I would never have to deal with her ever again, which left a huge smile on my face. In fact, as it turned out, that was the last time I ever saw Phyllis again.

About a year after my divorce, Faya and I began our life together with a huge wedding and honeymooned at Disney World. Having sold my rooming house to my mom and dad shortly after my divorce, Faya and I moved into a small apartment in a duplex that her mother owned. We occupied the bottom apartment, and her Mother occupied the top.

After 4 years we had finally saved enough to build a 3-bedroom ranch home in Racine, WI. Shortly after the house was finished, Faya gave birth to my pride and joy Tanya.

I was, and still am, the proudest father I could be. I remember working two jobs and still having time to pull her, and her little dashound Simba, around the neighborhood. She loved playing basketball with me when she got older, and was amazed the first time she actually beat me.

Faya worked two jobs as well, and soon we found ourselves drifting further and further apart. Eventually, after 29-years of marriage, we decided that we had lost the love that had once pulled us together.

Although some of the circumstances behind the divorce were similar, I think divorcing Faya was much harder on me then divorcing Phyllis. Not because of the years we had shared together, although I am sure that played some part of it, but because I knew how much it hurt Tanya to see her parents go their separate ways.

I can not say that I miss my life with Faya, but I will say that I will always and forever be grateful to her, for giving me such a beautiful daughter that has proved time and time again to be the greatest gift God ever gave me.

CONCLUSION

Today, when I look back at all the hell me and my fellow River Rats went through, I can't help but think about all that has happened to not only me, but to those around me.

I have not seen anyone from my Vietnam days in well over 30 years, but I still find myself thinking about them often, and wonder what their lives were like after they got back. I did maintain a friendship with Mike Bouballs for a few years after the war, heck I even went to his wedding. But as friends often do, we kind of drifted into our separate existences. I still think of him often, and would love to reunite with those men that meant so much to me back then, hell they still do.

I honestly feel that the bond that we formed while making our mark in the history books of fate, will forever tie us together, whether or not we see each other every day or by a chance encounter. Although seeing anyone of them again would be great.

As for my other family? Well Bryn did join the Marines, but as luck would have it, he became extremely ill and was unable to ship out with his battalion, that just happened to be the last group to be sent to Vietnam. He spent his entire military career safely between the shores of the United States. He and his wife Colleen now have four kids and four grandkids and couldn't be happier.

My brother Ross went on to college, by-passing the family military tradition, married a beautiful lady named Cathy, and had two kids of his own. Sadly, his wife died very young, and he is now raising his two kids on his own, but seems to be adjusting to his single parent role very well.

My father, who was always my gentle guiding light throughout my life, passed away in 2003 at the age of 85. I still miss him, but in a strange way I feel he is always watching out for me.

My Mom is alive and well, and has continued on with my father's work of enlightening her family to the ways of the Lord. The pain of losing dad is still with her I'm sure, but she never shows it. Instead she exhibits the strength of someone so secure in her faith, that she has helped all of us deal with our loss of such a great man.

My daughter has since, not only graduated college with honors, but is now a Nurse Practitioner on a maternity ward for a local hospital, and I could not be more proud of her.

I married my current wife Christine, in 2006 in a small tourist ghost town in Apache Junction AZ. She has one son and a daughter who has given us three grandsons that we just adore.

She was only 6 years old when I was in Vietnam, yet she has such a true appreciation of everything that I had gone though. She has not only helped me write this book, but she has guided me through the process of remembering those days in such a way, that I have somehow developed an even deeper understanding of what exactly we River Rats had truly accomplished.

I don't think this book would have been possible without her gentle guiding insistence. But more than that, she helped me remember such a trying time of my life, without causing any flashbacks or feelings of regret.

I would like to take a minute to thank my wife, who diligently spent two years researching, probing, and turning my random thoughts into such an honorable tribute to those great men.

My only hope is that by reading this book, people may realize what it meant to be a River Rat, and realize the sacrifices we made in such a horrific time in history.

May God bless each and every one of them?

GLOSSARY

A.T.C:	Armored troop carrier, 30 x 60 foot, 90 tons, capable of transporting 35-40 men. Hard top had chopper pad on bow. Ragtop did not. They had 2 diesel engines and were used on the narrow channels of the Mekong Delta.
B.G.:	Big guy that was associated with the anonymous group that shot two N.V.A prisoners off the front of our boat.
Boxcar plane:	A C-119 military transport aircraft used for transporting supplies and troupes into hot military zones.
Bow:	The front of a boat.
Bunker:	
Camp Pendleton:	Largest Marine training facility located 82 miles south of Los Angeles, CA.

Charlie: A word used to describe the North Vietnamese army and their allies.

Click: Military slang for a kilometer or .681 of a mile.

Hanoi Hilton: Hoa Lo POW Camp located in Hanoi Vietnam, famous for its brutal treatment of its prisoners

Hooch: A simple building constructed in war zones for housing military personnel.

In country: When you were in Vietnam or in an area away from the safety of a base you would say you were in country.

Knots: Speed measurement of 1 nautical mile per hour.

Mare Island: Decommissioned submarine base located in Vallejo, CA. Used for training incoming River Rats.

Mekong Delta: A narrow waterway off the Mekong river that branches off in many directions throughout South Vietnam.

N.V: The North Vietnamese that infiltrated the southern section of Vietnam, in hopes of integrating the communist ideas throughout the country, reuniting it under one government.

N.V.A:	North Vietnamese army that was specially trained by the Russians in hand to hand and weaponry combat.
P.B.R.:	Fiberglass pleasure boat with Jacuzzi jet pumps capable of reaching 25-29 knots.
Percussion Grenades:	Equal to 2 ½ sticks of dynamite.
Port:	Left side of a boat.
Sampan:	A flat bottomed wooden boat 11.5 to 14.8 ft long, used to transport goods up and down the Mekong Delta.
Sloughs:	A narrow channel of water 3.5 miles long and a mile wide.
Starboard:	The right side of the boat
Stern:	The back of the boat.
S.V:	South Vietnamese, mainly passive in nature, that we were asked to train in the art of warfare by their government, so they could maintain their peaceful lifestyle.
Treasure Island:	Military base located near San Franciso

ABOUT THE AUTHOR

Mark was a River Rat in Vietnam from 1969-1970. He shared life & death situation with man who he considered his extended family only to drift away from them once they returned home.

REFERENCES

Merriam-Webster Incorporated. (1993). Merriam
Webster's Collegiate Dictionary (10th ed.).
Copyright Philippines.

Page, T., & Pimlott, J. (1995). *Nam: The Vietnam
Experience 1965-75*. London: Orbis Publishing
Limited.